Showing Your Dog

Visit our How To website at **www.howto.co.uk**

At **www.howto.co.uk** you can engage in conversation with our authors – all of whom have 'been there and done that' in their specialist fields. You can get access to special offers and additional content but most importantly you will be able to engage with, and become a part of, a wide and growing community of people just like yourself.

At **www.howto.co.uk** you'll be able to talk and share tips with people who have similar interests and are facing similar challenges in their lives. People who, just like you, have the desire to change their lives for the better – be it through moving to a new country, starting a new business, growing their own vegetables, or writing a novel.

At **www.howto.co.uk** you'll find the support and encouragement you need to help make your aspirations a reality.

You can go direct to **www.showing-your-dog.co.uk** which is part of the main How To site.

How To Books strives to present authentic, inspiring, practical information in their books. Now, when you buy a title from **How To Books,** you get even more than just words on a page.

Showing Your Dog
A Beginner's Guide

ELAINE EVEREST

howtobooks

Published by How To Books Ltd,
Spring Hill House, Spring Hill Road,
Begbroke, Oxford OX5 1RX. United Kingdom.
Tel: (01865) 375794. Fax: (01865) 379162.
info@howtobooks.co.uk
www.howtobooks.co.uk

How To Books greatly reduce the carbon footprint of their books by sourcing their
typesetting and printing in the UK.

British Library Cataloguing in Publication Data
A catalogue record for this book is available from the British Library

ISBN 978 1 84528 368 1

Cover design by Baseline Arts Ltd, Oxford
Produced for How To Books by Deer Park Productions, Tavistock, Devon
Typeset by PDQ Typesetting, Newcastle-under-Lyme, Staffs.
Printed and bound by Bell & Bain Ltd, Glasgow

NOTE: The material contained in this book is set out in good faith for general guidance
and no liability can be accepted for loss or expense incurred as a result of relying in
particular circumstances on statements made in the book. Laws and regulations are
complex and liable to change, and readers should check the current position with the
relevant authorities before making personal arrangements.

Contents

Acknowledgements

I would like to acknowledge the help given to me in the preparation of this book from members of staff at the Kennel Club. Their support and understanding of dogs throughout the world is second to none.

I would not have written this book if it were not for the many newcomers to the hobby of dog showing that I have spoken to over the years who have been flummoxed by the strange world they have entered and have asked for a simple book to guide them.

Writing can be a lonely business and I wish to thank The Wild Geese, an international group of female professional writers of which I am a member, for their companionship and support.

Finally a big thank you to my friend and colleague Kelly Rose Bradford for her unstinting support and late night internet chats. This subject is alien to her but she truly needs to be owned by a dog.

Introduction

The Power of the Dog

There is sorrow enough in the natural way
From men and women to fill our day;
And when we are certain of sorrow in store,
Why do we always arrange for more?
Brothers and Sisters, I bid you beware
Of giving your heart to a dog to tear.

Buy a pup and your money will buy
Love unflinching that cannot lie –
Perfect passion and worship fed
By a kick in the ribs or a pat on the head.
Nevertheless it is hardly fair
To risk your heart for a dog to tear.

When the fourteen years which Nature permits
Are closing in asthma, or tumour, or fits,
And the vet's unspoken prescription runs
To lethal chambers or loaded guns,
Then you will find – it's your own affair –
But... you've given your heart for a dog to tear.

When the body that lived at your single will,
With its whimper of welcome, is stilled (how still!);
When the spirit that answered your every mood
Is gone – wherever it goes – for good,
You will discover how much you care,
And will give your heart for the dog to tear.

We've sorrow enough in the natural way,
When it comes to burying Christian clay.
Our loves are not given, but only lent,
At compound interest of cent per cent.
Though it is not always the case, I believe,
That the longer we've kept 'em, the more do we grieve:
For, when debts are payable, right or wrong,
A short-time loan is as bad as a long –
So why in Heaven (before we are there)
Should we give our hearts to a dog to tear?

Rudyard Kipling (1865–1936)

Rudyard Kipling sums up the feelings of a true dog owner perfectly. Puppies are a joy to own, but they grow up far too quickly. The years rush by and they're suddenly old and ready to say goodbye. It's important to spend our time wisely with our dogs, not just in grooming and feeding but sharing our hobbies as well. Dog showing is an ideal way to do this and to meet some interesting people and make dog-loving friends as well.

The pure breed canine world has taken a lot of flack of late by people who have no proper knowledge of our way of life or our dogs. Breeders and show people are being branded as uncaring and not fit to breed dogs. We have been blamed for every illness and every sick puppy in the land. Sadly those who choose to point the finger never take note of the good breeders, the breed clubs and the Kennel Club who are amongst the top canine enthusiasts in the world and at the forefront of canine care.

I'm pleased to see that the dog show fraternity are fighting back and will not tolerate the anti dog brigade who are trying to pull down our sport. Hopefully this will show the difference between decent dog breeders in the dog show world and the backyard breeders and puppy farmers who feed off this nation's love of dogs and breed for cash not soundness and temperament. In this book I have tried to convey the importance of buying a puppy wisely and from a respected breeder, where to find such a breeder and how to avoid the type of advertisement that will only lead to heartbreak.

I've owned dogs all my life. One of my earliest memories is of collecting our crossbreed (or mongrel as they were called back then) in my doll's pram and bringing him home. Butch was a maverick, all the local lady dogs used his services, he ran wild and free, as dogs did then – he broke all the rules, jumped fences six times higher than himself and had the most amazing fleas!

As an adult, and newly married, we owned a beautiful black Labrador cross Collie called Sabastian, who shared our lives for 14 years before leaving us and breaking more than a few hearts. My one true love is the Old English Sheepdog – commonly called the Bobtail. As I write this I am joined by one of the younger ones who wander in to remind me it's time for food or a cuddle. By my desk sit five wooden caskets; Oliver, Hayley, their daughter Gracie and her son Chuckie were all beautiful Bobtails and very much missed. The fifth holds the ashes of Oscar, our Polish Lowland Sheepdog – a truly individual dog.

Through my dogs I've met some wonderful people and made life-long friends. They've taught me about dogs and I've listened, absorbing their knowledge and passing it on in turn to people who have inherited puppies from my dogs.

You will see that I refer to the dogs in this book as 'he'. This is not to infer that I prefer dogs to bitches; it just keeps the delivery of information straightforward. Some of my best friends are bitches!

I hope you enjoy this book and that it helps you through the maze of rules and strange words that you will come across as you start out in the exciting sport of dog showing. Enjoy your showing and love your dogs.

I dedicate this book to the dogs that have been in my life, all the beautiful Paddipaws puppies we have bred and the owners who have taken them into their homes and their hearts. But I mostly dedicate it to my husband Michael who has been my long suffering chief groomer, puppy carer and driver to dog shows for many more years than either of us care to remember.

1

Starting Out

Before we go any further you must realise that not one single breeder in the world can guarantee that the puppy you take home will blossom into a show champion. Many things can go wrong along the way as your puppy grows, and perhaps he will end up too tall, too short, have the wrong type of coat or the wrong length of back. This does not make him a bad dog and he will most likely be a valuable member of your family, but his faults may not make him the high-flying winner that you expected. If however you have done your homework correctly and made the best purchase possible, at least you will have a good start to your new hobby.

BREED STANDARD

Every breed of dog that is registered in the UK with the Kennel Club has an official breed standard. This is a blueprint of how the dog should look and how he should move. All the breed standards are set out in a similar way and are updated when necessary. The type of things included in the standard are:

■ **General appearance**, **characteristics** and **temperament**, giving you a good idea of what the breed should look like plus its original use, and also whether the temperament is generally sound for the breed and for your family.

■ How different parts of the body should appear in the ideal breed specimen including **head** and **skull**, **eyes**, **ears**, **mouth**, **neck**, **forequarters**, **body**, **hindquarters**, **feet** and **tail**.

■ The breed's **gait** and **movement**.

■ The type of **coat** and how it covers the body and the **colour** required.

■ The **size** of dog and bitch, usually given as a minimum and maximum height.

BEING AWARE OF FAULTS

Faults are also mentioned as having to be considered when judging the dog. There is always ongoing work to improve the health of all breeds of dogs and some breeds do have certain health factors that are being watched. There are plans afoot to change breed standards to show more of these details although the Kennel Club, breed clubs and individual breeders will always discuss health concerns in the breed of your choice.

When visiting breeders to view puppies take a copy of the breed standard with you and ask the breeder to go over the points on the mother of the puppies and perhaps some of the other dogs. Any good breeder is only too pleased to give you guidance on this subject. They will also be more than happy to show you examples of points that are not so good – after all no one has yet bred the perfect dog. Perhaps they have a dog that is not quite as large as the norm or perhaps one that has the wrong ear set. Beware any breeder who tells you that every one of their dogs is perfect – they are kennel blind!

CHOOSING A DOG WITH SOUND TEMPERAMENT

When visiting a breeder you should be able to see the dogs and get a general idea of the temperament of their breeding. If the animals are snappy or very bad tempered do not listen to excuses, simply walk away. Visit a few dog shows and view the breed as it mingles with other dogs and people. If you already have a breeder that you are considering purchasing a puppy from, watch other dogs of the same breed and ask yourself if your potential puppy is as sound in temperament.

Visit a breed club show and introduce yourself to the committee and exhibitors – new members are always welcome. Tell them that you are looking to purchase a puppy and join the sport of dog showing. Many people will be only too keen to advise you and point out members who have puppies due. Be careful not to listen to gossip as there are always some who will try to cause trouble and blacken the name of a fellow exhibitor or breeder.

Never approach exhibitors when they are about to enter the show ring or are preparing the dogs, as they will be preoccupied with their work. Instead, approach them once they are back at their grooming table or bench and are more relaxed.

Purchase a copy of the show catalogue and watch the dogs in the show ring. Every exhibitor will be wearing a ring number that matches the number in the catalogue. If certain dogs catch your eye, mark your catalogue against the number and you will then have a record of the owner of the dog and the breeder for future reference.

CHECKING THE PEDIGREE

When talking to breeders who have litters of puppies ask them to send you a copy of the pedigree. A pedigree will show you quite a few generations of the dog's parentage and should also be marked with any health checks relevant to the breed. Hip scores, eye testing and other such details should be recorded.

You will also see some names in red or marked as champions. Do not be too impressed with a pedigree with umpteen champions listed. Yes, if they are in the ownership of the person selling you a puppy then you may be assured of a good puppy as they have bred and made them up to champions. Most stud dog owners will insist on only allowing use of their dog if the bitch is health tested and a suitable match, but sadly there are some that are only in the sport to make a quick buck to the detriment of the breed.

CONSIDERING THE TRAINING

Ask someone at the show if you can handle their dog – not in the ring of course! Walk it around, get a feeling for the dog and if it is controllable. Fancying a large Old English Sheepdog may be one thing but could you control him in the show ring and present him to the best of your ability? You will be attending training classes with your own puppy but to begin with take the opportunity to see if you can actually hold the breed you have chosen on a lead. No one will blame you if you change your mind – better to downsize your choice of dog before you pay for him and take him home.

PICKING THE RIGHT BREED

First and foremost, remember that whatever breed of dog you purchase it will be your family's pet and will spend many happy years living with you. Showing, or exhibiting as it is also called, is just a hobby and takes only hours each week of your dog's long life.

Having decided that you would like to try the sport of dog showing, you will have to choose which breed is right for you. With over 209 breeds registered with the Kennel Club there are plenty to choose from. Each of the breeds comes from one of seven groups. You may have seen these groups when watching the Kennel Club's Crufts dog show on television.

THE SEVEN GROUPS

The Working Group

This group consists of the type of dogs that work for a living, be it a guard dog or a search and rescue dog. You can be assured of a dog with a strong honest temperament in this group that includes:

Alaskan Malamute
Beauceron
Bernese Mountain Dog
Bouvier Des Flandres
Boxer
Bull Mastiff
Canadian Eskimo Dog
Dobermann

Dogue De Bordeaux
Entlebucher Mountain Dog
German Pinscher
Giant Schnauzer
Great Dane
Greater Swiss Mountain Dog
Greenland Dog
Hovawart
Leonberger
Mastiff
Neapolitan Mastiff
Newfoundland
Portuguese Water Dog
Pyrenean Mastiff
Rottweiler
Russian Black Terrier
St Bernard
Siberian Husky
Tibetan Mastiff

The Toy Group

Here you will find the smaller dogs. These are amongst some of the most popular breeds as they can fit into most homes and lifestyles and are both cute and sweet lapdogs that are still bold, even in their small packaging. They include:

Affenpinscher
Australian Silky Terrier
Bichon Frise
Bolognese
Cavalier King Charles Spaniel

Chihuahua (Long Coat)
Chihuahua (Smooth Coat)
Chinese Crested
Coton De Tulear
English Toy Terrier (Black and Tan)
Griffon Bruxellois
Havanese
Italian Greyhound
Japanese Chin
King Charles Spaniel
Lowchen (Little Lion Dog)
Maltese
Miniature Pinscher
Papillon
Pekingese
Pomeranian
Pug
Yorkshire Terrier

The Gundog Group

These are the medium to large breeds that were once trained to work to the gun retrieving game. Again some very popular upstanding breeds are to be found in this group including:

Bracco Italiano
Brittany
English Setter
German Longhaired Pointer
German Shorthaired Pointer
German Wirehaired Pointer
Gordon Setter

Hungarian Vizsla
Hungarian Wirehaired Vizsla
Irish Red and White Setter
Irish Setter
Italian Spinone
Kooikerhondje
Korthals Griffon
Lagotto Romagnolo
Large Munsterlander
Pointer
Retriever (Chesapeake Bay)
Retriever (Curly Coated)
Retriever (Flat Coated)
Retriever (Golden)
Retriever (Labrador)
Retriever (Nova Scotia Duck Tolling)
Slovakian Rough Haired Pointer
Small Munsterlander
Spaniel (American Cocker)
Spaniel (American Water)
Spaniel (Clumber)
Spaniel (Cocker)
Spaniel (English Springer)
Spaniel (Field)
Spaniel (Irish Water)
Spaniel (Sussex)
Spaniel (Welsh Springer)
Spanish Water Dog
Weimarana

The Pastoral Group

The Kennel Club split up the Working Group a few years ago when it had far too many dogs in the one group. The Pastoral Group are the breeds that once worked as herders for sheep and cattle and their double coats ensured they could work in the severest of weathers. Dogs in this group are loyal faithful breeds to own and include:

Anatolian Shepherd Dog
Australian Cattle Dog
Australian Shepherd
Bearded Collie
Belgian Shepherd Dog (Groenendael)
Belgian Shepherd Dog (Laekenois)
Belgian Shepherd Dog (Malinois)
Belgian Shepherd Dog (Tervueren)
Bergamasco
Border Collie
Briard
Catalan Sheepdog
Collie (Rough)
Collie (Smooth)
Estrela Mountain Dog
Finnish Lapphund
German Shepherd Dog (Alsatian)
Hungarian Kuvasz
Hungarian Puli
Komondor
Lancashire Heeler
Maremma Sheepdog
Norwegian Buhund

Old English Sheepdog
Polish Lowland Sheepdog
Pyrenean Mountain Dog
Pyrenean Sheepdog (Long Haired)
Samoyed
Shetland Sheepdog
Swedish Lapphund
Swedish Vallhund
Welsh Corgi (Cardigan)
Welsh Corgi (Pembroke)

The Terrier Group

This group includes the feisty smaller dogs originally bred for hunting vermin. These dogs can be a handful to train and control but are a joy to own and are much loved by families. They include:

Airedale Terrier
Australian Terrier
Bedlington Terrier
Border Terrier
Bull Terrier
Bull Terrier (Miniature)
Cairn Terrier
Cesky Terrier
Dandy Dinmont Terrier
Fox Terrier (Smooth)
Fox Terrier (Wire)
Glen of Imaal Terrier
Irish Terrier
Kerry Blue Terrier
Lakeland Terrier

Manchester Terrier
Norfolk Terrier
Norwich Terrier
Parson Russell Terrier
Scottish Terrier
Sealyham Terrier
Skye Terrier
Soft Coated Wheaten Terrier
Staffordshire Bull Terrier
Welsh Terrier
West Highland White Terrier

The Hound Group

This is a fine group of dogs originally bred for hunting by sight or sound. Many breeds in this group require a substantial amount of exercise. Breeds in the Hound Group include:

Afghan Hound
Azawakh
Basenji
Basset Bleu De Gascogne
Basset Fauve De Bretagne
Basset Griffon Vendeen (Grand)
Basset Griffon Vendeen (Petit)
Basset Hound
Bavarian Mountain Hound
Beagle
Bloodhound
Borzoi
Cirneco dell'Etna
Dachshund (Long Haired)

Dachshund (Miniature Long Haired)
Dachshund (Short Haired)
Dachshund (Miniature Short Haired)
Dachshund (Wire Haired)
Dachshund (Miniature Wire Haired)
Deerhound
Finnish Spitz
Foxhound
Grand Bleu De Gascogne
Greyhound
Hamiltonstovare
Ibizan Hound
Irish Wolfhound
Norwegian Elkhound
Otterhound
Pharaoh Hound
Portuguese Podengo (Warren Hound)
Rhodesian Ridgeback
Saluki
Segugio Italiano
Sloughi
Whippet

The Utility Group

This is a very mixed group of dogs and tends to hold the breeds that do not fit into the other six groups. Mainly non-sporting breeds, the group includes:

Akita
Boston Terrier
Bulldog

Canaan Dog
Chow Chow
Dalmatian
Eurasier
French Bulldog
German Spitz (Klein)
German Spitz (Mittel)
Japanese Akita Inu
Japanese Shiba Inu
Japanese Spitz
Keeshond
Korean Jindo
Lhasa Apso
Mexican Hairless (Intermediate)
Mexican Hairless (Miniature)
Mexican Hairless (Standard)
Miniature Schnauzer
Poodle (Miniature)
Poodle (Standard)
Poodle (Toy)
Schipperke
Schnauzer
Shar Pei
Shih Tzu
Tibetan Spaniel
Tibetan Terrier

QUESTIONS TO ASK YOURSELF

■ The size of dog you wish to own is an important point to consider.

■ If it is a large breed, are you strong enough to control him?

■ Will you be able to walk him on a lead let alone handle him in the show ring?

■ The cost of his food bills and medical expenses will also be higher than that of a smaller breed, as will grooming and bedding equipment. Can you afford this?

■ Where will your dog live and sleep?

■ Do you have room in your home for a big dog and more importantly will your family be happy to share their home with say a St Bernard or an Irish Wolfhound?

■ How about your age? A dog can live for 12 to 15 years, will you be too old to exercise and care for him by the time he is elderly?

■ Are you prepared to spend around £25 each week on your dog? This is what it can cost to own a larger breed before you even contemplate show costs.

HOW MUCH TO PAY?

Regardless of the quality of your puppy, you will find that during its life it will cost the same amount of money to feed, insure, train and show. In fact if you compared the daily running costs of a crossbreed, a mongrel, a 'designer dog' or a top quality show dog of a similar size you will find that their day-to-day running costs would be very similar.

Therefore, when investing in a dog that you wish to exhibit around the country do not stint on purchasing the best dog you can afford. That is not to say that you couldn't find a good example of your chosen breed amongst a litter bred by a pet owner, but it is best to remember that by going to someone who knows their breed and breeds to the requirements set out in the Kennel Club standard for that breed you will be off to a better start than relying on your own judgement and that of someone who is not so knowledgeable about the breed.

By purchasing from a breeder you will also have a link to their knowledge and back up throughout your dog's life, in both its home life and its show career. You will also find that you have made a life-long friend within the world of dogs.

Expect to pay from £500 upwards for smaller breeds with many middle-sized and larger breeds costing around £1,000 each.

DOING YOUR RESEARCH

Visit dog shows that are arranged by clubs of your chosen breed. The Kennel Club can supply a list of the recognised clubs. Most will organise dog shows, pet events, talks and seminars for their members. When attending these events make yourself known to the club's committee members and tell them that you are looking for a suitable puppy and that you wish to exhibit him. The secretary of the breed club will be able to advise you on the price to pay for a show puppy.

This research will be your first tentative steps into introducing yourself to fellow exhibitors – people you will meet at shows around the country most months of the year. You will see these people more than your family. In fact many of these people will become your family and will play a part in your life until the day you die. Births, marriages, illness and death are all shared in the canine community, as we are all one big happy family. Like family, some of us will fall out at some time and some people make enemies. This is all part of the colourful world of dog showing.

Watch the dogs that are being shown and take note of their owners' and breeders' names in the show catalogue. When the owners are not preparing for the ring speak to them about their dogs and your plans to join them as an exhibitor. It may take a while to do this research but at the end of the day you will have found someone who will put you onto their list of owners when they next have a litter of puppies. All the people you speak to will give you an idea of the price of a puppy and you can begin to save your money.

BUYING FROM ADVERTISEMENTS

Avoid buying your puppy from advertisements seen in newspapers, pet shops and newsagents' windows. Can you really expect to find a well-bred, healthy dog from an advert than runs alongside a second-hand motorbike or a vacancy for an office cleaner? Would someone who had carried out all health checks on their brood bitch, selected a good stud dog and devoted time and care to a litter of puppies then pay 50 pence to put a card in a shop window to sell their valued brood? Nine times out of ten they would not have done so.

A GUIDE TO FINDING A PUPPY FOR THE SHOW RING

As a novice in the world of dog exhibiting you may not have many contacts in the show world. If you are fortunate to have a friend or family member already enjoying this sport they will be able to point you in the direction of a good breeder. Let us assume, however, that you have no idea where to purchase your chosen breed. Here is a guide on how to track down a puppy for the show ring and a breeder you can trust.

Finding known breeders

Contact the Kennel Club and ask for a list of people with puppies that are currently on their lists. If you have access to the internet, you will find that on the Kennel Club's website each breed is listed individually with sections for each area of the country. If you do not have access to the internet, request a list through the post. Email: www.the-kennel-club.org.uk Telephone: 0870 606 6750

Before you pick up the telephone to contact any of the listed breeders you need to know that they are known breeders for the show ring. Unfortunately puppy farmers and backyard breeders still get their breeding onto the Kennel Club list, although every attempt is undertaken to stop them by concerned breed clubs and breeders.

You next need to contact the breed club of your chosen breed. Many breeds have more than one club, most have a designated area of the UK to cover and quite often there is a national club as well. The Kennel Club has a list of every breed club in the United Kingdom as they have to register with them in order to organise shows and other breed events. Once you have the details of the breed clubs, telephone the secretary of the club covering the area of the breeder you are interested in and ask them if they have knowledge of this breeder and would they recommend purchasing a puppy for the show ring from this person.

Most breed clubs also keep a 'puppy list' of members who currently have puppies for sale. Ask for a copy of the list but you must make sure that the secretary knows that you intend to show your dog. While you are speaking to the breed club secretary ask for a membership form and join their club. Even before you purchase your puppy you can begin to get involved with the breed, and attending events and receiving club newsletters will break you into the sport gradually.

The dog show world is full of rules, words and customs that to begin with you will find quite alien. But, by immersing yourself early on, you will soak up this knowledge and start to become part of the world of dog showing.

Visiting a breeder

Start to telephone the breeders on the list that you have complied. Try to ring at a reasonable time of day. You will be keen to make contact but early morning will find the breeder feeding and mucking out puppy pens – you would be surprised how much mess a little puppy can make over night so think what six, seven or even eight can make! Mid morning onwards would be best. Prepare a list of questions to ask, but remember that this person could well become someone you are in contact with for the next ten years, possibly even more, so start by being friendly and introducing yourself rather than firing off a barrage of questions.

Tell the breeder something about yourself and why you want to show one of their puppies.

Ask if the dam and sire (that's mum and dad to you) can be seen when you visit. Quite often the sire of the puppies will live in another part of the country – even overseas with the introduction of the pet passport and also with breeders being able to purchase semen for artificial insemination from anywhere in the world.

Ask about the health of the parents and if the breeder has certified proof of these documents and if he or she can post or email a copy of the pedigree for you to read.

Ask when the puppies are ready to go to their new homes and when you can visit to meet them. Do not be too pushy here; most breeders will not let anyone – even family – in the house for a few weeks in case of infecting the little lives they are caring for.

Ask if they work with the breed club and if they judge. You need to build up an overall picture of these people and how committed they are to dogs in general.

Tell them that you are a novice exhibitor and ask if they will be able to guide you through the maze of rules that are so daunting to new exhibitors. If you find that this person is not able to do so, think again about purchasing a puppy from them at this time.

Make an appointment to visit the breeder and take down details of their email address so that further contact can be made easily and without taking up too much of their time. Perhaps send a message afterwards confirming your conversation.

This conversation is probably the first of many with someone who will become a friend for the rest of your life.

You should be able to visit the breeder several times to see the puppies and with their help decide which puppy is best for you. Your new breeder will teach you how to groom and care for the puppy and you will learn many valuable points about the breed during those first few weeks.

Travelling to find your puppy

Be prepared to travel quite a distance when looking for a puppy for the show ring. Some breeds are low in numbers and this means that you will have to do a little more research than you would for some of the more popular breeds. Hopefully you will find a lovely puppy from a show kennel within 20 or so miles from your doorstep. Others will have to travel to the other end of the country in their search.

Author's story

❝ *It is quite common when planning to have a litter of puppies for people to hear about you and request that their name be put 'on a puppy list' to wait for a puppy. Breeders tend to work down the list and if we have more names than puppies we will pass them on to another breeder that we would personally recommend.*

I had one gentleman on my list some years ago who was, to put it politely, overly keen to have a puppy. Once I had notified him that the bitch had whelped he was on the telephone several times each day and every time he wanted to know when he could visit. Each time I pointed out that I never let anyone near the puppies until they were at least four weeks old and even then they had to go through a decontamination process before getting near my little babies. This would fall on deaf ears and, yes, he kept on ringing. He wanted to know how high on the list he was and to have the pick of the litter; his demands grew by the day. Eventually, when the puppies were a mere two weeks old and when he rang to say he was on his way to see them, I flipped. I pointed out that he could not be allowed in the house to which he insisted I should hold the puppies up at a window so he could pick which one he wanted.

Needless to say this chap never got to see my puppies let alone purchase one and it was some days before I lost the feeling that I was being stalked and my husband was allowed to leave me alone in the house! Talking to fellow breeders around the country (yes we all talk to each other), I realised that he was doing the same to a friend in the Midlands and also to a friend in Wales. It was very creepy.

Part of breeding a litter and finding good homes is working with your gut instinct. If you are not happy with a prospective buyer simply say you do not have a puppy for them at this time. I have done this on numerous occasions and can safely say that our puppies all end up in happy homes.

Once you have met the breeder and the puppies please take your name off any other list you may be on so as not to disappoint other potential purchasers who are also looking for that perfect puppy.

When purchasing a puppy ourselves we have travelled quite a long way from our home in Kent. Oliver came from Merseyside and Hayley from the West Midlands. Both came from breeders who were excellent at keeping in touch with their puppy owners and helping them in their future show careers. Both sets of breeders became good friends that we stayed in touch with.

A good exhibitor. . .

Researches where to find a good breeder and learns about the breed. They will join a breed club, read books and visit shows to start the long process of learning what is involved with owning their chosen breed.

A bad exhibitor...

Will pester a breeder, assume they know best and think that any dog can be shown.

2

Learning to Show

TRAINING AT HOME

Training for the show ring starts the day you come home with your new puppy. Of course you are going to want to pet and fuss over this beautiful bundle of fluff, but in between the cuddles and kisses lay down some ground rules that will put you in good stead for the day you enter the show ring when your puppy is six months old. Start to train your puppy from the day he arrives home by encouraging him to stand correctly and have his feet and head examined and he should not have a problem when starting his show career at the age of six months in the minor puppy class. You will be able to smile as you stand at your first dog show with your obedient and calm puppy, observing other puppies refusing to cooperate with the judge when they are faced with their first show.

VACCINATIONS

Make an appointment to see your vet and have your new puppy checked over. Depending on his age your puppy may have had his first vaccinations and be due for the second dose. As a rule, young puppies are vaccinated against canine distemper, leptospirosis, infectious hepatitis, parvovirus and kennel cough. Usually these vaccinations are given in two doses two weeks apart but your vet will be able to advise you about this procedure. At this stage your puppy will be too young to take out for walks or mix with other dogs, so training must be started at home.

GROOMING

All dogs should be able to lie on their sides whilst being groomed. You do not want to be struggling with a large dog to hold him down each time you need to brush his coat.

A grooming table is an excellent purchase. Buy one that has a ridged rubber table top as it is non slip, hard wearing and can be cleaned easily. Most tables have collapsible legs and can be carried in the car to dog shows – it is easier to groom on a table than on your knees on the concrete or muddy floor at a show ground! Purchase a grooming table that has wheels and doubles as a trolley. It will be invaluable on show days and can carry a large amount – ideal for that sack of dog feed bought at the show. There are different shapes of grooming tables to accommodate all sizes of dog.

Whatever surface you intend to groom your puppy on, place a comfortable piece of blanket or a thick towel down first before picking up your dog and laying him down. You may need to be firm but try not to frighten him. If you use soothing words and a firm hand, he will soon realise there is nothing to fear.

Run a soft brush over his coat before turning him over and repeating the process. This should only take a few minutes at this stage. Relaxed dogs tend to sleep while being groomed and your puppy will soon get into this habit.

Next check his ears and eyes for signs of wax or dirt. Use the words 'ears' and 'eyes' so he learns what to expect. Teeth also need to be inspected as this is done by the judge at every show to check the dog's bite. Use the command 'teeth' and lift the gums gently to look at the teeth. You could also start to use a dog tooth cleaner so that once the adult teeth come through he is used to his teeth being cleaned.

Finally, check your puppy's feet. Look between the pads and trim off any excess hair that may matt and accumulate dirt. A dog's feet are always checked at the show and if your puppy gets used to this examination as a baby he will not bat an eyelid once he is in the show ring.

Once his short grooming session is finished, lift him down from the table and give him plenty of praise – perhaps even a titbit as a reward. Performed daily, this short session will give you and your puppy confidence in the future when he is expected to be handled by strangers in the ring.

INTRODUCING A COLLAR AND LEAD

Most puppies are not keen on the feeling of a collar around their necks and will not be happy when first made to wear one. Purchase a soft puppy collar to begin with rather than a hard leather one and leave it on a notch looser than needed until he ignores it completely.

In the show ring you will be using a different type of lead to exhibit your dog. Normally this is no more than a soft cord with a loop for the neck that is tightened with a small clasp. Use this to train your puppy to walk indoors or in your garden. Loop the lead around his neck and encourage him to walk on your left-hand side. This is how your dog will be shown so it is advisable to always walk him on your left-hand side from day one. You may need someone in front of you to begin with to call the puppy forward so that he is not aware of being guided by a lead.

If you are able to train him to walk beside you in a straight line and perhaps even practise a 90 degree turn left or right, then you will have achieved enough to be ready for your ringcraft training classes once he is allowed out in the wide open world.

When walking your dog in the street or park do not use the show lead as it will not give you the control of a collar and lead. Also, it is a requirement by law that every dog wears a collar and lead and a tag showing his owner's details in case he is lost. If you take your dog to a park or open field, use the opportunity to practise your ringcraft training. If this becomes part of your dog's life it will not be such a culture shock when show day arrives.

When going out for a walk always carry several plastic bags in your pocket to pick up after your dog. If there is not a bin bring it home with you. Do your part in giving the dog world a good image.

HANDS ON

Hopefully by now you will have visited a few dog shows and begun to see what happens when your dog is examined by a judge in the ring. This is known as 'going over a dog' and will become a major part of your dog's showing life. Judges are very tolerant of young puppies and will allow for them being wary or lively. But as the dog progresses to the next class for junior dogs it will not go down well if he does not want to be touched by the judge. This could make the difference between being placed or 'thrown out' – another frequently used term that means not being placed.

When you have visitors to your home or when you stop to talk to people in the park their first instinct will be to want to pat and cuddle your cute puppy. This is not a problem but your dog must learn that not all people who touch him want to play. Asking visitors to act first as a judge would and run their hands over the dog's body and check his teeth, eyes and ears while you hold him steady would help greatly in his training. Your friends may not know why they are doing this, but the puppy doesn't know that and will soon be used to being 'gone over' by a judge. Afterwards by all means let your friend have a cuddle with the puppy and let him play like any other dog.

FUN TIME

Distinguish between fun time and training. Never let your dog play tug of war with his lead – that is for training. In fact try not to play tug of war at all as it could damage a young jaw that is still growing.

Similarly if you have a coated breed, care should be taken that any rough play is not damaging and ripping out his coat or your dog will look very silly when exhibited up against other dogs with a well cared for appearance. Sadly some judges do not look further than the outer appearance of a dog so do not give them the opportunity to place you further down the line – in other words giving your dog a fourth or fifth place when he really deserved a first!

Puppy classes

It is likely that your vet runs their own puppy socialisation classes. These are an excellent way for your little dog to meet others at an early stage and realise that there are other dogs out there in the big wide world. He will be able to interact with other dogs and meet strangers and know how to deal with them.

You will meet fellow puppy owners who live locally to you and who could become fellow dog walkers for years to come. There may also be the chance of meeting other owners who are hoping to show their puppies. Car sharing to shows and training classes is not only a cost-saving opportunity but also provides company and friendship when driving hundreds of miles each weekend.

Ringcraft classes

You will need to attend a ringcraft class. This is not optional for a novice exhibitor – both you and your dog need to be trained. After you have had several dogs you may decide not to attend classes, but even then your dog will need to be trained.

Do not be tempted to attend an obedience club instead as the training is completely different and not intended for the show ring. In the ring your dog needs to move on a loose lead away from your side so as to show off his movement and outline. In obedience training he will have to move closer to your side and sit when told to. A show dog must not sit but stand and show off his outline. By all means when your dog is older try obedience classes, agility, flyball or even dancing to music, but at the moment your dog needs ringcraft training in preparation for his show career.

If you have not met someone who attends such a class in your area, contact the Kennel Club for a list of registered clubs. Your breed club may also be able to advise you on a class or club in your area. If there is one that is frequented by others in your breed then all the better as some breeds are shown slightly differently and you will be able to pick up hints and tips from them.

Most ringcraft classes are held weekly and will cost between £1 and £2 per dog to attend. There is often a yearly club membership fee of around £10. This is money well spent for the advice and training you will receive. Each week you will be shown how to stand your dog and how to move him. This is exactly as you would do in the show ring. Different people will go over the dogs and if you have any problems there will be expert handlers who can help you overcome them.

The secretary of your ringcraft club will always have schedules for dog shows on their table. These will be general open shows that are being held at local show grounds. When I say local I mean within about 20 miles – we travel a lot in the dog show world! Take a look at these schedules to see if there are classes for your breed. If not, don't be disheartened as you can enter a not separately classified class. Just make sure that your puppy is old enough for the show before you get excited. He needs to be six months old on the first day of the show. Do not worry if he is too young as there will be another show along shortly.

You will meet many people at these classes who will be long-time breeders, championship show judges and complete novices like yourself. These are the people you will bump into at shows and who will become an integral part of your showing life. You may never learn their names as they will be known as 'Fido's mum' or 'the sheepdog lady' but even so they will wave to you across a busy show ground or hold your dog lead when you need to dash to the loo.

MATCH NIGHT AND PARTIES

Apart from the weekly classes, there will be match nights when a judge will be invited to judge the member dogs. This is practise for them and for you, and the whole event is organised just like a proper show. There may be prizes, no doubt a raffle, and you will gain valuable experience of how to prepare for and enter a show albeit on a small scale.

Dog folk enjoy a party and your class will celebrate Christmas and other events along with their dogs. Fancy dress and games are enjoyed by all participants once the serious business of ring training has been completed.

Author's story

❝ *As a judge I love to go over a puppy and see the future of the breed when it first starts out. To have a well behaved six-month-old puppy in front of me is a joy rather than a struggle! I also like to speak to the owners afterwards about their puppies. I still remember all those years ago when were out with our first puppy and being spoken to by the judge after she had finished judging. She walked along the show benches and stopped to pat our dog and wish us well with her. It didn't take much for her to do this and to this day nearly 40 years later it has stayed with me.*

We have attended some wonderful ringcraft clubs over the years. One was very local to our home and was ideal for our Old English

Sheepdogs. However, when we wanted a class for our Polish Lowland Sheepdog we travelled for an hour to Brighton each week as we knew the instructor there was experienced with this particular breed.

Remember that the club is not there as an extension of your social life but to train your dog. So if you find your puppy is not flourishing under the guidance of a club then move to another – but be prepared to travel.

A good exhibitor...

Will start to train their dog from day one and will attend ringcraft classes at the earliest opportunity.

A bad exhibitor...

Will not bother to train their puppy at all and will expect the dog to perform perfectly when he steps into the show ring.

3

Grooming and Presentation

After months of ring training and getting your puppy to the peak of perfection you must consider his grooming. Yes, you already brush him through and keep him clean but preparation for the ring is a completely different thing altogether.

MAINTAINING A HIGH STANDARD OF CLEANLINESS

All dogs should be clean and well presented every time they enter a show ring. It is an insult to the judge to give them a dirty dog to go over. Also, it's not fair on the dog to be in a dirty state at any time.

You will notice that judges have wet wipes or a bowl of soapy water on their table in the ring. This is so that they can clean their hands if they handle a dirty dog. How embarrassing would it be for you if they stop to wash their hands after touching your exhibit? Not only will fellow exhibitors have noticed but breed enthusiasts from outside the ring will be watching as well. No doubt many will be looking up your ring number in their catalogues to see who owns the dirty dog. Things like this stick in the world of dogs and many years later you could be known as the person with the dirty dog.

Your dog should be free of knots and matts and smell sweetly.

GROOMING PROCEDURES

Depending on the size of your dog and the length of his coat, you will have to formulate a grooming plan so that you are prepared for the show ring. For larger hairier breeds this can begin two or three days before a show and take some hours. Set aside time for grooming so that you are not stressed and rushed when preparing for a show. If you keep on top of your grooming it will not be a big task before the event.

DO IT YOURSELF

Where possible you should be preparing your dog for the show ring yourself. There is no enjoyment in sending a dog to a grooming parlour, however good they are. You need to know how to prepare a dog for the ring and not to rely on other people.

When you first start your research into your chosen breed read as much as possible about coat care and how to prepare a dog for the show ring. A bath and brush through is ideal for the family pet but with many breeds the coat needs special care if it is to be kept in tip top condition for the ring. Some dogs need a harshly textured coat so bathing could ruin the condition for many months. Attending breed-related workshops and seminars will give you advice on your breed's coat care for the ring.

COAT PRODUCTS

Visit any dog show or browse the pages of canine publications and you will be amazed at the myriad of products available to wash into coats, spray onto coats and rinse out of coats. They are well packaged, beautifully perfumed and cost a bomb. These products claim to soften coats, harden coats, clean coats, stop coats breaking, help coats grow, keep coats white and keep coats black. The only surety is that if you fall for what is written on the bottle it will keep you poor!

Speak to fellow exhibitors in your breed and you will find that many use a basic shampoo, even a baby shampoo available from the supermarket, and then nothing more than water sprayed onto the coat to settle any static.

If your breed is picked for random coat testing at a show and your dog has to give a coat sample you will be penalised for having any product in the coat that could alter its natural colour or texture. Any award won at the show will be taken away from your dog, which can prove to be embarrassing and costly as the expense of showing your dog that day would have been wasted. This practise does not set a good example for dog exhibitors as it is tantamount to cheating.

BATH AND BLOW DRY

If your dog's breed has a long or thick coat the likelihood is that you will need to use a hair dryer after each bath. Introduce your dog to a dryer at an early stage so that he doesn't have a fright come show day. Start by drying your own hair around the puppy and letting the warm air waft around him. Once he is used to the noise and warmth use the hair dryer on his dry coat while he is being groomed so he trusts you and becomes familiar with the equipment.

If bathing and drying your dog is to be a big part of your show presentation you might progress to one of the many industrial-sized dryers to be seen on trade stands at dog shows. Training your dog to lie down and be groomed from an early stage will make your show preparation so much easier.

CLIPPERS AND SCISSORS

Some breeds' coats are clipped and styled for the show ring. Unless you are confident working with clippers never attempt to use them as a slip can cause damage that will take months to recover from. If you need clipper training there are courses regularly advertised in the canine press. It is tempting to trim a dog to shape using your scissors but in most breeds the coat is plucked and not trimmed with scissors at all. Ask your breeder to show you the grooming techniques needed for your breed. When visiting shows watch the exhibitors as they prepare their dogs and learn from them.

GROOMING TABLE

A good grooming table is worth its weight in gold. To be able to groom at waist height on a stable surface saves much back-breaking work and the dog is much happier. Purchase a table that fits the size of your dog when it is lying on its side. If you purchase one that has wheels fitted to the underside it will double as a trolley when going to shows.

Rather than lifting a heavy dog onto the grooming table, place a chair beside the table and encourage your dog to climb onto it. There are also grooming tables with hydraulic systems to lower the table down for the dog to climb on with ease – very handy for elderly dogs and exhibitors with bad backs.

GROOMING EQUIPMENT

Grooming equipment varies from breed to breed. Terrier owners will use stripping knives whereas owners of longer-coated breeds might rely on good quality bristle brushes and wide-toothed combs. You really need to watch exhibitors at dog shows to see what is used for your breed. If a dog is groomed at home ready for the show you will not need to carry too much to the show with you.

EARS

It is strange how so many exhibitors forget to clean their dogs' ears or remove excess hair from the ear canal. If you make this part of your grooming routine your dog will have less chance of getting an ear infection from the build up of wax. There are many products on the market for ear cleaning. Powders, drops and wet wipes are available, but whatever you use do not dig into the ear canal or subject your dog to a painful experience. When removing hair from the ear use tweezers and try to be gentle or your dog will not thank you.

TEETH

Keeping your dog's teeth clean should be a daily task and not left to the day before the show. Bones and hard biscuits should keep the teeth free of tartar but if there is a build up you may have to ask your vet to scrape the teeth. As this procedure is carried out under anaesthetic, try some of the products on the market first such as doggy toothpaste or a powder that is added to a dog's food – some are remarkably efficient. Anaesthetic should only be used for emergency procedures.

MOUTH

While checking and cleaning your dog's teeth also check his mouth. Not only can the coat get knotted around the lips, collect debris and cause pain, but if there are folds of skin there can sometimes be areas of infection. Trimming the hair and wiping with a gentle lotion containing aloe vera will keep the area fresh. A judge will always look at a dog's mouth so not only should it be clean but the dog must be used to being handled around his face.

Some dogs have wet mouth and slobber quite a bit. Carry a dry cloth to wipe your dog's face and keep him dry. There are towelling bibs available and breeds such as St Bernard can be seen wearing them on the show ground.

FEET, NAILS AND PADS

Judges will often check dogs' feet so make sure they are clean and tidy. Any hair between the pads should be trimmed away as it can collect tar, mud and stones and cause lameness – and is very painful.

Nails should not be overly long as they will not only impede movement but also show that a dog is not being exercised properly. If your dog is used to being walked on grass and soft ground try to do some pavement walking as this will naturally wear down the nail. If you use nail clippers go very carefully and do not cut off too much nail as you could cut the quick and cause the nail root to bleed and become infected.

Before trimming away excess hair on the outside of your dog's feet, check that this is done in your breed as you do not want to change the expected outline of your dog in anyway. It is amazing how a short piece of coat snipped off in error can take so long to grow again.

Dog clothes

After all the days of grooming and preparation you open your front door on the morning of the show to find it is raining. Drive to the dog show and the whole show arena is a quagmire. Rather than risk running your dog through the rain, and hoping he jumps the puddles of mud, be prepared with coat and boots for him and for yourself. Having a lightweight shower-proof coat complete with leg coverings and also a set of boots will ensure that you get to your bench with a beautifully clean dog.

The day of the show

Once you are at the show you will need to have a quick brush through and check that your dog still has clean ears, clean teeth and a clean face. Silly as it seems, a damp face cloth wiped around the dog's mouth and a light dusting of chalk, corn flour or potato flour rubbed in will be enough to clean him up. Remember to brush out all of the flour before entering the ring.

It is amazing how some people are still doing a thorough groom through at the ringside. Yes, some heavy coated breeds do need more care but you will see people working on dogs from scratch with less than an hour to go to start of judging. Some dogs will not tolerate being over handled before being shown as it unsettles them in the ring. By the time your dog is old enough to start his show career you will both understand each other and you will know how he copes with grooming and show presentation.

Once you have been in the ring and have finished exhibiting for the day give your dog's coat a brush through to remove any snags that may have been caused by fingers running through his hair while being examined. Then it is time for a bowl of water and a pat on the head for another show well done.

COAT TRIMMING

Walk round the grooming areas of some breeds and the floor is covered with cuttings where dogs have been trimmed. Not only is this frowned upon as it alters the shape of a dog artificially, but to leave the evidence on the floor for all to see is foolish. Keep your grooming area clean and if there is not a bin nearby for hair and other waste put it in a bag and take it home with you.

POO BAGS

You will be surprised to see many people frantically looking for a bag as their dog is defecating on the ground. That is not the right time to realise you are bag-less! Always carry a plentiful supply of bags, put them in your coat pockets, your show bag, the car and the pocket of your show outfits. Either recycle supermarket carrier bags or purchase scented nappy sacks – you can get loads for only £1. Set an example to others – after all the eyes of the world are on show dogs these days just waiting for us to make a mistake. Never give anyone reason to point their finger at you and brand you a bad dog owner.

Author's story

❛ *We all have grooming tales to tell and there are several that still make me chuckle. We had groomed our large puppy Oliver to within an inch of his life and he went into the ring and won his class. Being a lovely summer's day we sat ringside with a cold drink to watch the other classes and to be ready to go back into the ring with the other unbeaten dogs for the challenge. Oliver was, we thought, laying quietly under our chairs in the shade snoozing. He was safe as we had hold of his lead. As we called him out to go into the ring we realised why he was so quiet, he had found a discarded tea bag and had chewed it to pieces. Never had we worked so fast (or broke out in such a sweat) as we tried to brush the tea leaves from his face that day.*

My most favourite memory is again with Oliver when we stayed in a motel the night before a championship show. Ollie lay on his blanket on the floor and I watched Luciano Pavarotti in concert on the television as I groomed. The next day Ollie won his class and qualified for Crufts – his first qualifier. I marked the memory three years later by calling his first son Paddipaws Pavarotti, who turned out to be a most handsome boy and a credit to his breed. As I write this Dylan, as he is named, is living in Lincolnshire approaching his fourteenth birthday with his devoted owners, the Fordham family (Cloudnine Old English Sheepdogs) and enjoying his retirement.

A good exhibitor...

Plans their time to groom their dog for exhibition and never uses products that alter their dog's coat. They carry plastic bags just in case and make sure that they are great ambassadors for their breed.

A bad exhibitor...

Leaves grooming waste around their bench at shows and never picks up after their dog.

4

Entering a Show

PLAN AHEAD

As your dog's ring training progresses you will need to start looking towards entering your first proper dog show. Apart from companion dog shows that can be entered on the day, all other shows have to be entered weeks, sometimes months, in advance. This is so that the catalogue can be made up for each class and breed entries, and so that benches, ring layout and awards can be prepared. Consequently you should start planning your show entries months before your puppy is six months old and ready to start his show career.

FINDING A DOG SHOW

Through the canine press

The first place to look for forthcoming shows is in the weekly canine press. By now you will have been reading them on a regular basis and will have spotted that the show advertisements are to be found at the back of the paper. Breed club shows are also discussed within the breed columns so remember to check them on a regular basis even if to begin with you are not sure what everyone is talking about! The large adverts are always for championship shows and premier open shows.

If your puppy will be six months old on the first day of the advertised show, and you feel that you are ready for your debut, contact the show secretary and request a copy of the schedule. In these modern times it is becoming more frequent for the show society to have a website and an email address so try to use this to contact the secretary as they do have day jobs and a home life and cannot be expected to be at home to answer every telephone call. You may even be able to download a copy from their website which will save the secretary's time and the society's bank balance.

Read the breed notes that are printed in the canine press. The correspondent's report on news from breed clubs will tell of shows that are nearing the deadline for entry. You will also see adverts in this section for breed club shows around the country. Try to enter these shows as they are a way for you to get to know your breed and the people who are involved with it.

Through breed clubs

If you belong to a breed club you will receive a copy of any show or event they are organising. Try to support your breed clubs as there will be times when you need their help and guidance and the profit made from their shows contributes to funding telephone help lines and rescuing dogs in need.

Gradually as you have entered more shows you will find that schedules drop through your letterbox even though you have not requested them. This is because your name is now on a database of exhibitors from previous shows and the society is inviting you to enter once more.

Through printers

There are three companies that between them print many of the show schedules and catalogues in the UK:

■ Canine Information Directory: www.canineinfo.idps.co.uk

■ Fosse Data Systems: www.fossedata.com

■ Higham Press: www.highampress.co.uk

These companies now provide a service whereby you can download schedules direct from their websites rather than going through the organising society or club. These schedules are listed many months ahead of each show so are worth bookmarking.

Results from the shows are also published on the websites at the end of each day's judging of major championship shows. This is a great boon to those who would like to know the results of the judging but are unable to attend the show. In years gone by we would have had to wait for news from a fellow exhibitor or the main awards that were published in the canine press the following Friday.

WHAT IS A SHOW SCHEDULE?

The organising club of every dog show has to provide a schedule of the classes being held at the show. This schedule is presented to the Kennel Club and is set out in accordance with their guidelines. It will come to you as an A5-sized booklet. The cover will show the name of the society, the date of the event, the address of the showground and the deadline for entries.

Classes

Inside will be a list of the classes broken down into breeds. If the show is being judged under the group system the breeds will be listed under their respected groups. Under each breed you will find a list of classes. These will range from minor puppy up to the open class and can be for mixed or single sexes. The number of classes for each breed depends on the size of the show and the show committee's decisions based upon previous entries. If you find that your breed is not listed do not despair, as there will be classes called 'not separately classified' for any dogs without a designated class. There are also variety classes where you can enter as long as you have entered your breed class.

Judges

The names of the judges will be listed next to the classes and you may find that you have what is called a breed specialist who is someone who has owned and shown your own breed and only judges that particular breed. Or you may have what is called an 'all rounder' who is someone that is qualified to judge many breeds. Both types of judge will know how to assess your dog and will be aware of the breed standard for your own breed.

These judges will have been invited to judge at the show perhaps several years before the day of the event as it can take a long time either to have the judge passed to perform their duties or to have them free to judge at that time. Many societies will not invite a judge to assess a breed if they have done so in the previous year or two. This ensures that there are a variety of judges in each area of the country.

When not to enter

Sometimes you will find that your breeder is judging at a show. Do not under any circumstances enter your dog as it is poor sportsmanship. Also if someone has been helpful to you and handled your dog in any way do not enter under them as it does not look good to other exhibitors and will take the shine from any place that you are awarded.

You cannot enter under members of your own family – but that is obvious, isn't it?

By all means make a complimentary entry, that is make an entry but in the box for class number write 'complimentary'. Although you will not actually take part in this class, your complimentary entry will show your support for the judge and will also contribute much needed funds to the show society.

Rules

You will see a long list of rules about the show. Take time to familiarise yourself with them as they are rules set by the Kennel Club and if you fall foul of them you will pay the penalty later by having an award removed or even being fined or banned from showing. Most of the rules are sensible and you will see why they are needed as you progress through your show career.

WHICH CLASS TO ENTER

To begin with, being faced with a list of classes will seem very confusing. But you will find an explanation for each of the class names listed in the schedule under the heading 'Definition of Classes'. There can be many varieties of class names but here are a few of the most common:

Minor puppy: Dogs that are six months and not exceeding nine months on the first day of the show.

Puppy: Dogs that are six months and not exceeding 12 months on the first day of the show.

Junior: Dogs that are six months and not exceeding 18 months on the first day of the show.

Yearling: Dogs that are six months and not exceeding 24 months on the first day of the show.

The above are known as age classes. If you accidentally enter the wrong class the secretary is allowed to move you to the right one if it has been scheduled. If it hasn't, you will be moved to the open class with the older dogs.

Post graduate: Dogs who have not won a challenge certificate, five first places at championship shows in post graduate or higher classes, such as in limit, open and so on, for the breed.

Limit: Dogs that have not become show champions under Kennel Club rules or won seven firsts in limit or open class for the breed.

Open: This class is open for any dog of that breed to enter.

Note that you would look silly entering your puppy of six months into a class that is higher than yearling as he would be competing up against much older dogs, perhaps even champions of your breed at some shows.

Start your puppy's show career by just entering one class or two at the most. You will find competing in the ring can be quite stressful and tiring, and so could your young puppy. This could upset him for any future shows and sometimes even put him off showing for life.

If you are keen to enter every class then good luck to you but remember that you are the one who will look silly if the judge places you very low down the line of winners in the puppy class and then ignores you in the higher classes. Yes, you can choose not to go into the class, but you have to notify the ring steward that you wish to do so.

COMPLETING THE ENTRY FORM

The entry form must be completed properly. A mistake on the form could cost you your win at the show if it is proved that you entered wrongly. As well as writing your name as the owner of the dog along with your address, you must complete the section about each of the dogs that you enter.

To begin with, have your Kennel Club registration document in front of you so that you copy the details correctly. It has not been unknown for someone to enter the wrong dog and lose a place because of it. You will need to give your dog's full pedigree name, his breed, sex, full date of birth and his breeder's name. Next you need to write in the names of his sire and dam (the names of his father and mother). Finally you must write in the class number or name of the classes you wish to enter.

Write clearly and in capitals so that the person compiling the information from the entry forms does not make a mistake that could affect your entry on the day.

You have to sign the declaration part of the entry form. This is a very important section and you must read it and not just blindly scribble your signature. You are agreeing that you will be bound by Kennel Club rules – remember all those rules you were going to read but never got around to? Perhaps now is the time to read them! You are also agreeing that your dog is healthy and has not had any operations to change his natural conformation. This is a serious document and you must be honest when you sign it.

If completing your first entry forms seems confusing ask someone to help you. Your breeder will be only too pleased to help but if he or she is not able to ask at your ring craft class. Eventually this form filling can be done in your sleep but until then check and double check what you have written before writing the cheque and putting it in the post box.

Technology is such that it is now possible to enter a dog show online and pay online as well. In much the same way that you keep records of postal entries do the same for your online entries. Cross-reference this with your bank statement in case there is a query at a later date.

Note that show societies are not impressed with people who bounce cheques when making their entries. Not only does it create extra work for the administrator but it is also costly to the show society and to you in bank charges. Most societies fine exhibitors and names of people with unpaid debts are listed in the Kennel Gazette and they are penalised by the Kennel Club.

To begin with, you will be entering only age-related classes but as time progresses the classes your dog exhibits in are determined by how many wins he has achieved. Consequently it would be better to wait and enter closer to the cut-off date (which is clearly shown in each schedule) so that your entry reflects your dog's true achievements.

Meeting the entry deadline

Take note of the close of entry. If you miss the deadline you have missed the chance to show your dog. As long as your envelope is dated by the postal sorting office on or before the last date of entry, it will be accepted. Mark your calendar so you don't forget – better still, send it in early!

Receiving proof of entry

If you would like proof that your entry arrived with the show secretary, enclose with your entry form a stamped postcard addressed to yourself which can be posted back to you as your proof of entry. Remember to write the show details on the card otherwise you will not know who has sent it back to you!

Passes

Only the large general championship shows send passes in the post to all entrants. These are usually your car park pass, catalogue voucher (if you have ordered one), ring numbers and any other relevant news. You need these passes to get into the show so do not lose them or leave them at home. In fact, when the paperwork drops through your letterbox staple it to the show schedule so that all documents for that show are kept together.

Breed club championship shows and general open shows do not, as a rule, send out passes. To ensure that your entry has been received, enclose a stamped addressed postcard with your entry.

This is then signed and returned by the show secretary and can be used as your proof of entry.

Establish a system

It is a good idea to have a system when entering dog shows as you will be entering many shows and need to be able to lay your hands on the relevant documents. Purchase a box file and put all the schedules at the front in order of the date of close of entries. That way, the schedule at the front of the box will be the next in line to be posted.

As you enter a show write the details of your entry on the front of the schedule and move it to the back of the box file in the order of show dates. Also make a note in your diary as to the show and entry details.

Any paperwork sent to you about the show can then be added to the schedule, paper clipped if necessary. Sometimes you may come across information about road closures or motorway repair work that may hinder your journey. Cut it out of the newspaper and add it to your file.

When packing your show bag, transfer the schedule to the bag so it is not forgotten.

Keep a list of your dog's places at the shows along with the name of the judge. Not only do you need this as you progress to higher classes, it is also interesting to look back and see how you fared under the judge if his or her name comes up at another show in the future.

There can be lots of interesting information inside a show schedule so take time to read each one thoroughly. It is worth holding onto any special schedules such as those that celebrate anniversaries or have had last minute changes because of some national incident. These become collectors' items in years to come and will also bring back memories of your first days in the show ring.

Author's story

❛ *Keeping records of which shows we've entered becomes second nature but even then we can make mistakes. I have a friend who travels alone to shows with her dog and during a busy show season she crossed the old Severn Bridge towards South Wales. Stopping for a coffee at the first services on the Welsh side, she started to read the schedule only to realise to her horror that she should have left the M4 motorway and travelled north on the M5 as the show was at the Three Counties showground in Malvern. At the time, she was campaigning her dog for his Junior Warrant and needed only a few more points. Meanwhile he was fast approaching the award's cut-off age of 18 months. She reached the show by the skin of her teeth and won her points.*

Another friend used to take her caravan to the shows and often stayed the weekend. Travelling north to one show they set up camp and had a leisurely afternoon sunbathing and enjoying a barbecue in the evening. Entering the showground the next day they found that they had missed their breed judging as it had been scheduled for the previous day.

I've never missed a dog show but I once had a worrying moment when my cheque for my Crufts entries was returned as I had forgotten to sign it. Luckily the office was forgiving and our entry was still accepted. Because of a simple mistake I could have missed out entering the most important show in the dog show calendar!

If you are as forgetful as I am, I suggest you either ask someone to check your entry before it is posted or design yourself a check sheet to make sure you have done everything correctly.

A good exhibitor...

Keeps show records in order and reads them before a show.

A bad exhibitor...

Misses shows or has awards taken away for not completing paperwork correctly.

5

Travelling with Dogs

TRAVELLING BY CAR

Once the dog showing bug has bitten, you will find that much of your time is spent travelling to and from shows. It stands to reason that you will need a reliable car in which to transport yourself, the dog (or dogs) and the amazing amount of equipment that is needed just to show even a small dog. Many show goers prefer estate cars or vans but, with the expense of petrol and considering the green factor, it is possible to travel to a show with a smaller car that conserves petrol and helps save the planet.

DOG SAFETY IN CARS

If your car has room for a cage, fit the strongest one available in the rear section. Make sure that it is not only secure but that it will stay in place if your car rolls during an accident. Not only will your dog be safe during the journey but if he is used to a cage at home he will happily settle down to sleep in an environment that he knows.

Smaller cars may not have room for a cage, however your dog must still be made safe while you are driving. Not only can he be injured if your car is hit but it is possible he himself could injure you if he is catapulted forward during an accident. Dog safety harnesses can now be purchased in sizes to fit all dogs. These harnesses clip onto the seatbelt fixtures on the rear seats and keep the dog safe during the journey.

CAR TRAINING

Do not leave it until the day before the show to check if your dog enjoys travelling in your car. This outcome is never good and you are liable to have a dog that dribbles and is sick (or worse) during the trip. It is not fair to take a dog to a show in this condition. The trip should be enjoyed by you and your dog otherwise he will not be his best in the ring and neither will you.

Start early with your dog by taking him for a drive around the block or to the shops. Have someone sit with him just in case he is upset to begin with. If you drive to parks and places where he can walk and play, he will identify the car with arriving at an interesting destination and very soon car journeys will become enjoyable.

A dog that does not travel well can be a problem as there will be times that he needs to visit the vet or be taken somewhere urgently and you will then face a mighty problem that only sedatives will cure. No one wants ever to have to sedate a dog unless it is vital!

TAKING OUT A BREAKDOWN SERVICE POLICY

No one wants their car to break down but it is always the case that when it does on show day you are hundreds of miles from home. There are plenty of breakdown services available so you can easily find one to suit your pocket. You need to be covered for the eventuality that your car cannot be repaired roadside and therefore needs to be towed home.

Read the small print before paying for a policy and check that whoever you go with gives you written assurance that they will transport your dog as well as you in the case of a breakdown. There have been many instances of tow truck drivers refusing to have dogs in their trucks and the poor animal being kept in the car as it is towed behind the truck.

ARRIVE IN TIME

You need to calculate your journey and add time for hold ups along the way. A reliable map is well worth the money, especially if you do not know the area that you are travelling towards. Satellite navigation equipment is all well and good for main roads but with many shows being off the beaten track your journey could be eventful if you rely on these electrical gadgets for some of your show journeys. Use the teletext service on your television to check on motorway delays before you leave home.

Tune into local radio stations as you travel so that you stay alert as to possible delays up ahead. Some car radios have the facility to alert you to problems on the roads in the area of the local radio station.

KEEP IN TOUCH

With mobile phones being part of our daily lives, it makes sense to keep one with you while travelling so far from home. Programme it with simple names that can be understood such as home, mum, dad, vet and neighbour. If you are injured, and cannot use the phone yourself, whoever helps you can easily tell who the numbers belong to on your phone.

DOGS ON BOARD

When packing your bag the night before the show, take a few minutes to write on a postcard that there is a dog travelling in your car. List his breed, name, age, colourings and any other useful information such as whether he is microchipped or has tattoo identification. Stick the card to your dashboard so that it is on view at all times.

If you are involved in an accident it is likely that a dog could break free and run away in fear. We hear of this happening several times each year. Sadly some dogs are killed on motorways while others run wild for weeks before capture. If the emergency services and fellow drivers know there is a dog loose, a disaster can possibly be averted.

LEAVING DOGS AT HOME

It is possible that you will sometimes attend a show and leave a dog at home alone. Try to arrange for a neighbour or friend to pop in to let him out and generally check that he is well. But if something should happen to you what will happen to this dog? Would he like to be alone for days on end before someone realises? Use the postcard idea again to show that there are pets at home and give contact details of a key holder who can care for them until your return. Knowing that you have taken every precaution possible for your pets will ease your mind if something delays your journey home.

PREPARING FOOD AND WATER

When setting out early in the morning – and especially when you start showing in earnest – you will find that you are on the road long before the birds are out of their nests and the sun has risen. Your dog may be used to having a meal first thing in the morning but to feed him that early could have serious consequences while you are on the road. Try to make stops every hour of your journey so that your dog can stretch his legs and do his business. Just as you would pack food for yourself to eat during the day, try to pack small packets of food for your dog. Small amounts given often are better for his stomach than his usual one or two meals. Perhaps feed him some dry biscuits in case he is still prone to car sickness.

It is possible to purchase plastic water bowls with lips that stop the water spilling from the bowl during a journey. Although it is better to have proper water stops, these types of bowls are a godsend on hot days when you are held up in traffic. Always pack water for your journey as it may not be readily available during stops or at the show. There have been shows where the water is fed above ground to temporary water stations and the water has heated in the hot sun – not very pleasant for the dog and many refuse to drink warm water.

USING SEAT COVERS AND BLANKETS

As a dog owner you will no doubt have a plentiful supply of bedding for your dog. If your dog is travelling on the rear seat of your car you will need a protective car seat cover. It is possible to purchase made-to-measure covers but although these types of covers protect the seats they will be hot for your dog. Try to use old sheeting and towels that will absorb moisture and keep a dog cool during long journeys. In colder weather pack plenty of the type of blankets used on vets' beds that can be used by your dog and any passengers if the weather becomes very bad.

STAYING OVER

You will visit many beautiful parts of the United Kingdom during your show career but, strangely, most of the time you will see a field full of dogs and show rings before heading home on yet another concrete motorway. Signs to local beauty spots and places of interest will grab your attention, but you will never have time to stop and look. So why not make a weekend of your travels and see a little of the country around the show venue?

Show schedules often have a list of hotels that accept dogs but these can be booked up very quickly. Try contacting the tourist office closest to the venue and find out about the smaller bed and breakfast accommodation that accepts dogs. These are often delightful places to stay and you will find that the property owners are very interested in your dog, his wins and your interesting hobby. While other exhibitors are driving through the night to reach the showground, you will be enjoying a full English breakfast before taking a short and leisurely trip to the ringside.

KEEPING YOUR ROOM CLEAN

No matter how careful you are, there are bound to be dog hairs left in the room that you rent. If you carry a bed sheet with you, it can be thrown over the bed and will protect the bedding and your sanity. Saying that, do not let your dog onto beds and chairs in any room that you rent. Think of those who will use the room next – they may not be so keen on the odd stray dog hair. Most rooms have en suite facilities and dogs are attracted to these as the floor is usually tiled and cool. Check there is nothing interesting for your dog to chew or demolish before retiring for the night.

A packet of wet wipes, a small aerosol can of furniture cleaner and a hair removal brush in your grooming bag are ideal companions in case you need to do a quick clean up job in the room before vacating it. Leave a window open to freshen up the room or squirt your dog grooming spray around to leave it smelling fresh. By taking a little care when staying anywhere with your dog you will be invited back and you will not make a bad name for dog owners, the majority of whom do clear up after their pets.

TRAVELLING BY CARAVAN AND CAMPING

Many show goers travel with their own caravans, camper vans or tents. With a lot of major championship shows taking place in the summer months and there being facilities near showgrounds to stop over, it is becoming increasingly common for exhibitors to travel from one show to the next and use their holiday leave to attend dog shows. Show schedules will include details of camping grounds in the area if there is not one adjacent to the showground. As exhibitors wind their weary way home after a long hot day at the show, many hundreds will be firing up the barbecues and opening bottles of wine to celebrate or commiserate their day at the dog show. It does sound very tempting.

HOT DAYS

It is surprising how hot a car can become as the sun rises in the sky. Never be tempted to leave your dog in the car when you stop for a break on your journey to the show. Even with a window left open the car can turn into an oven and there are many instances of dogs dying from the extreme heat. Any journey taken with a dog onboard must be planned with care. If the dog cannot go into a cafe or service station with you take him to the picnic area and enjoy a meal in the open air with him. Even sitting on the curb by the side of the car or under a tree in a car park is better than leaving your beloved dog to die an awful death.

During your journey try to keep your car cool for your dog. Leaving windows open in the front of the car may frighten him with the force of the wind rushing through the vehicle. If you do not have air conditioning fitted in your vehicle, purchase a few solar-powered fans for his cage or the back seat. These are inexpensive gadgets that clip to the car window and are very effective.

Silver blankets left over the car while you stop at the show will reflect the heat away from the inside of the vehicle and keep it cool enough to climb into when you leave for home.

ADVERSE WEATHER

It is possible to hit really bad weather during your journey. Snow and storms can be just as horrendous as days that are too hot. Not only do we have to take care of our own comfort at these times, we also have responsibility for our dogs. Packing coats and wellington boots, a small shovel and a flask of coffee can make all the difference when held up in a blizzard. Similarly a dog coat and dog boots mean that you can walk your dog to safety away from the car in the coldest or wettest of situations. It is possible to purchase small kettles that run off of your car battery. Having this and an emergency pack of dried milk, tea, coffee, sugar and some dried soup or noodles can make all the difference when you are wet, tired and cold.

MAKING PLANS FOR THE JOURNEY

As travelling around the country attending dog shows becomes second nature, you will soon know what to take and what to leave at home. Plan for your journey and allow plenty of time to get to the show and plenty of time to drive home. Enjoy your days out and make the journey part of the day trip rather than a means to an end. In time, you will find interesting places to stop for a rest and also places to avoid. Enjoy your trips to the dog shows as all too soon, as your dogs grow old, they become just distant memories.

Author's story

⟨ *It is always the way that when you are furthest from home a once reliable car breaks down. This happened to us once as we drove from Kent to the West Country for a breed championship show. We cruised to a halt on the busy motorway with thick black smoke belching from the engine. Grabbing hold of our dog William, we climbed over the metal railing at the side of the motorway to stand and wait for the rescue service. William didn't flinch although I shook every time a lorry thundered by and whipped the wind around our faces. It was so noisy we could hardly hear ourselves think.*

Eventually a rescue van arrived and, after much head nodding and tutting under the bonnet of the car by my husband and the rescue man, we were told the engine was dead and we had to be towed home. I did ask if we could be taken to the show first (we were five miles from the venue) but my husband was horrified that I had even asked the question. Our contract would only take us one way – home! At the time, there were some awful stories doing the rounds about tow trucks not accepting dogs and them having to travel alone in the car as it was towed. As it was, the truck that arrived was driven by a delightful man who fell in love with William – well, who wouldn't? – and who insisted he had the best seat in the truck.

It was a long journey home and at one point the man pulled into a service station. I was dying for a cup of tea but, no, he had stopped for his new mate 'Bill' (William) to stretch his legs and share a sandwich – we did not exist! Needless to say, we arrived home with a defunked vehicle, hot, hungry, tired and fed up, whereas William hopped from the truck stuffed full of cheese and tomato sandwiches, wiggled his butt at his new friend and bounded indoors! Who says it's a dog's life?

A good exhibitor...

Plans their journey considering their dog's comfort and safety.

A bad exhibitor...

Never considers the heat or a comfort stop when travelling with their dog.

6

The Day of the Show

It is finally here: your first dog show – the day you have groomed, trained and prepared for over the past months. You will be nervous; that is understandable. Your trepidation can manifest itself in many ways: frequent trips to the bathroom, feeling nauseous, snapping at the children and being grumpy with your partner are just some of the common symptoms. However anxious you feel, try not to let your nerves creep down the lead to your dog. Dogs are very clever. They can pick up any change in the family routine and will be quick to realise that this particular day is going to be very different from his normal routine.

Right up until the minute you leave home keep your dog's routine as normal as possible. Let him go outside to do his business and take a walk if he usually does early each morning. If you have a long journey ahead of you, it may be sensible not to feed him before the journey unless you have time to exercise him and let his stomach settle otherwise there could well be a nasty mess in the car later.

COPING WITH BAD WEATHER

If it is raining or if the ground is still covered in frost or dew, put boots and/or a raincoat on your dog before exercising him as the last thing you need on entering the showground is to have to wash your dog's feet before he goes into the ring. Most dogs enjoy wearing boots or a raincoat but purchase yours early (leaving room for growth) and make sure he is used to wearing the garments so there isn't a fight to get him into them before the show. If you arrive at the show and find the ground muddy, carry the dog if he doesn't have boots or a coat. Plastic bags of any kind can be tied around his feet to keep them clean in an emergency.

Don't forget that you too will need wet weather clothing. Wellington boots and a raincoat that folds up small are ideal and can be left in the car ready for the wettest of weather. A thermos flask of coffee is a good idea as it is most welcome when you cannot find a service stop that accepts a dog on the way to the showground. A cup of tea at your bench before leaving for home is also welcome and costs little compared to some of the catering establishments found on showgrounds. Many exhibitors now carry their own food as it makes sense to save money where possible when you have a fairly expensive hobby to fund.

KEEPING CLEANING PRODUCTS TO HAND

There are cleaning products available that can be used without water to clean a dog's coat. So if you find yourself before a show with a muddy dog or a messy rear end, use a no rinse product to clean the area, dabbing it semi dry with kitchen paper before rubbing in corn flour or potato flour to soak up any excess liquid. Once the powder is dry brush out the coat and all should be as before – clean and shining.

Some exhibitors go so far as to carry battery-operated hair dryers, the type that are used for holiday travel. These are excellent for longer coats but make sure your dog is used to these noisy gadgets or he will freak and be a nervous wreck even before he goes into the ring.

Remember that you are breaking Kennel Club rules by using any product to enhance a dog's coat, so if you are unsure about the cleaning product use water instead. A plant mister filled with water is just right for adding water to the coat without soaking the whole area.

COPING WITH HOT WEATHER

You may think that a hot day is ideal for travelling and spending outside at a dog show – wrong! Your first consideration must always be your dog and his requirements. A car can be very hot and if, as frequently happens these days, you are held up in a traffic jam how will you keep him cool? Air conditioning is now available for many makes of cars so try to have this facility for your dog. A shaded area of the vehicle with a cool breeze is also ideal.

You will find, amongst the stands at major shows, various items that can keep your car and dog cool on the hottest of summer days. Silver reflective blankets are very handy for pinning across car windows to keep the inside of the vehicle cool while it is parked. Use another to shield your dog if you are sitting ringside in the heat of the midday sun. Battery-operated fans that fit onto dog cages cost only a few pounds are such a boon to the exhibitor, as are fans powered by a solar panel that can be clipped to your car window.

If a dog becomes overheated he must be cooled down and you need to seek veterinary advice. There are vets on hand at the major shows and on call for smaller shows. Wet towels laid over the dog's back will go some way to cool him down but you must seek the help of a vet as soon as possible. A dog can show overheating in several different ways: he will pant profusely, appear sluggish and even unresponsive. Some dogs will be sick or perhaps collapse. Eyes and gums can appear very red. At this stage a dog can die within minutes of heatstroke so obtain veterinary assistance immediately.

CARRY DRINKING WATER

Always carry your own drinking water for your dog. It may be that you are not near to a tap at the show or when you stop for a break in your journey. The size of your dog depends on how much water you need to carry, but have enough just in case you need it to wash muddy paws or your own hands.

When planning to travel on hot days, three-quarters fill an empty lemonade bottle and place it in your freezer the day before you travel. The water will then slowly thaw during the day so that you have cool drinking water. Never give your dog ice cold water to drink on hot days as it could cause cramps and bloat.

Some dogs are not keen on the drinking water at the showground so a plentiful supply from home can be useful for those fussy dogs.

NAVIGATING CAR PARKS

When attending larger dog shows you will be allocated a car parking ticket. Sometimes you have to prepay these and it is worth doing this as the charge is usually higher on the day of the show. Gradually, as you visit showgrounds around the country, you will get to know the best and the worst places to park. You will also learn that you need to get to the shows early in order to secure a car park near the show entrance. It is not unusual to have to walk a long distance from your car to the show entrance and then to your tent or ring.

You will have a dog (or dogs), a trolley, bags and entry paperwork to juggle, let alone the odd child or family member who has joined you for the great adventure. Add driving rain or unbearable heat and you will begin to realise why getting to a show early is the aim of many show goers.

WHERE TO GO

Once you are out of your car, have unloaded your gear and headed for the show entrance, you will need to know two things:

1. Where your ring and bench are situated

2. Where to collect a show catalogue

Both of these items can be found just inside the entrance. If you are attending a large show, there will be show officials situated inside the entrance who are only too pleased to point out where you should be heading. At smaller shows there will be a sign on the wall showing the ring layout and where each breed will be judged.

Also nearby will be at least one table where catalogues can be collected. Try to pre-order a catalogue as they can run out on the day of the show. Also, by paying in advance the catalogues can be a lot cheaper.

BENCHED SHOWS

Most general championship shows are benched. This means that for every dog entered there is a bench provided for him to sit on and rest. The bench is made of wood so you will need to carry a rug for him to sit on. There is also a chain especially designed to clip to your dog's collar and onto the ring on the bench so he cannot escape. There is room under the bench to stow away bags and other items and nearby will be a grooming area for your grooming table. These benches are numbered, and the number is the same as the one you will wear into the ring. This number is unique to you for that show.

Benches are laid out so that each breed is kept together and the numbers run numerically and alphabetically. You will find yourself benched next to others with the same initial as yourself and your dogs will be of the same breed. This enables you to quickly make friends with your near neighbours.

There is a Kennel Club ruling that dogs should be kept on their benches apart from being groomed, exercised or shown, but this is a very grey area that many people seem to ignore.

SHOW SAFETY

Never leave your dog alone on the bench. Sadly there are a few unscrupulous people about who may tamper with your dog. Also, your dog may get very distressed at being left alone and bark and howl, upsetting other exhibits and exhibitors. It has been known for young dogs to get so upset that they damage the benching area and become unfit for the show ring. If you are travelling alone there will be times when you need to leave your dog so try to find someone in your breed who will hold your dog's lead and keep an eye on him. You will be able to reciprocate the favour and this is yet another way to make friends with fellow breed enthusiasts.

FINDING YOUR BEARINGS

Once you have settled your dog on his bench and given him a drink of water, you need to get your bearings. Take a look at your catalogue to see how many dogs are entered in your class and also double check the order of judging. It will become an important part of showing to check who you are up against in your class at each show. You may find yourself competing against a high-flying dog and sometimes it may be that you are with dogs that you have beaten in competition. Whoever is in your class, remember that each show has a different judge and every dog is judged on his performance that day so keep on your toes at all times.

Sometimes you are the first breed in the ring and other times you will be waiting a few hours before your breed is called. Check out where the ring is. You can exercise your dog at the same time, but keep an eye on the clock. Dogs are always judged before bitches in every breed and puppies are judged first, so if you have a puppy you must be ready ringside at the allotted time. If you arrive late it is possible the judge will refuse your entry. That would be a sad beginning to your show career.

PREPARING YOUR DOG

Back at your bench have a cup of tea and get your dog ready. Check he has not picked up any dirt on his coat and that his eyes, ears and teeth are clean. If he is from a long-coated breed you may need to groom him through and prepare the coat for the ring.

Other breeds just need a quick flick of the brush and a check through and they are ready to go.

Swap his collar and lead for his show lead and clip your ring brooch to your shirt or top. Your ring number is always placed on your bench at the larger championship shows. At smaller open shows and breed shows you will be given your ring number as you enter the ring for your class. Practise clipping this piece of card to your ring clip as it can be very tricky sometimes if you are a little nervous and are also holding a frisky dog. If you are having problems ask someone for help – we were all beginners once and most people are only too happy to help a newcomer.

You may have a long wait before your class so take your dog for a walk so he can relieve himself and stretch his legs. He will get to know where the noises are coming from and not be so startled by strange noises and sights when he is in the ring.

PRESENTING YOURSELF

What is the point of spending your time grooming your dog and keeping him in tip top health if you are going into the ring dressed like a slob and letting him down? You would be surprised how many people show a dog wearing scruffy jeans and shabby shirts.

Remember that you will be bending over a dog and running around the ring so pick your show clothes carefully. Women in high heels, mini-skirts and low tops may attract some judges but this won't get you far in your show career. Similarly, men with low-slung jeans resembling builder's bums are not an attractive sight. When showing a dog you are simply doing that – showing off your dog. This means you are exhibiting your dog to the best of your ability; your clothing forms a backdrop to your dog and its colours should compliment him.

Unless you have a black dog, a pair of smart black trousers and a clean shirt in black or white are perfectly acceptable. Coloured blazers and jackets have been popular for a few years now and if you decide this is for you then make sure they are machine washable! Never wear trousers or skirts that are the same colour as your dog as he will not stand out clearly when being exhibited. Think of your clothing as a backdrop to the dog; it should complement the dog's colouring as well as make the exhibitor look smart.

Shoes should not have heels or make a noise when you move. Soft trainer-style shoes that are comfortable to wear and will not harm your dog if he should run under your feet are easy to find and should be a staple part of your wardrobe. Most exhibitors have two wardrobes: one for showing and one that is not for showing – you can guess which one is worn more.

Choosing your underwear

Well-endowed women should check that they have a comfortable bra to wear when showing, as the only movement that should be on view is that of the dog and not the female owner.

Men also: remove keys and loose change from your pockets before entering the ring. If a judge spots money flying in his or her direction as you move your dog around the ring, they will think it is a bribe!

ENTERING THE RING

Be ready at the ringside for when your class is called. This job is done by the ring steward who is there to make sure that the right dogs enter the ring and to make the judge's job as easy as possible. The steward will call the class and check that all exhibitors are present before handing over to the judge. You will be directed to the side of the ring to await the judge. This is the moment when all those months of ring practice click into place. You've done this next part umpteen times in practice and chances are you are more prepared than some of the other competitors, so be reassured. Keep an eye on the judge at all times and follow what he or she indicates.

Try not to be at the front of the line up when you enter the ring as that way you can settle your dog and also see what is required of the exhibitor as they go in front of the judge. Do not fuss over your dog but on the other hand do not let him play – he is here to work. When the judge indicates for you to step forward, take your time to set up your dog either on the table or the ground depending on your breed. Listen in case the judge asks you a question such as the age of the puppy. Answer with a smile and do not start a conversation. This is strictly taboo.

Move your dog as directed and take your time. This is the moment when you own the ring for a few minutes. Use it all and try to keep your dog on a loose lead as he moves. So many nervous exhibitors string up their dogs so the front feet cannot touch the ground. When the judge has finished looking at your dog they will say thank you and you must return to the end of the line up.

Once all dogs have been seen, the judge will walk along the line up and possibly indicate for a few dogs to move once more. You need to watch the judge all the time and also keep your dog standing correctly. All at once the judge will point to the winners – usually five – so don't miss the moment they point to you.

The steward will be standing in the middle of the ring so walk to where he or she indicates as you may be first, second, third, reserve or very highly commended. Set your dog up once more as the judge may change their mind. Once the place cards and possibly rosettes are handed out, wait in line as the judge may need to write a critique of your dog. They will then thank you and you are free to go.

You are on show from the moment you enter the ring to the moment you leave it – win or lose. There could be other judges observing your breed from the ringside and bad sportsmanship will be remembered. Remember to keep a smile on your face and congratulate the winners.

SEEN DOGS

If you have entered more than one breed class you will have to go back into the ring to compete. You will be classed as a 'seen dog' and the steward will line you up with other 'seen dogs' away from the unseen dogs waiting to be assessed. Before deciding on the class winners, the judge will look over your dog once more and hopefully call you in as one of the chosen five winners in that class.

It can get tricky as classes progress and more dogs become 'seen', as the steward and judge must make sure that no unbeaten dog is placed below a dog he previously beat in an earlier class – very tricky but you will soon learn how it works.

BEST OF BREED

Once all the dog classes have been judged, the steward will call for all unbeaten dogs (class winners not beaten in another class) to enter the ring to compete for the Challenge Certificate or Best of Sex. This means you, if you won first place in your class. You will be told to line up with the other dogs and may be asked to move your dog once more. When the judge has decided on the best dog they will award a Challenge Certificate and also a Reserve Challenge Certificate.

There is also an award for Best Puppy Dog and on this occasion that could be you. Quite often you will have to run around the ring to do a lap of honour to the applause of fellow exhibitors and the dogs will join in barking excitedly.

You will realise from this process that if you ever win a class you must keep your dog clean and tidy as he has to go back into the ring once more.

When all the bitch classes have been judged, your judge for the day will pick their Best Bitch in the same way that the Best Dog was chosen. Following this, the dog and bitch will re-enter the ring to compete for Best of Breed. You will then be called to compete for Best Puppy in Breed against the bitch puppy and the chance to represent your breed in the puppy groups later in the day.

OPEN SHOWS

If your first show is a smaller open show it is possible that dogs and bitches are in the same class, in which case the winners of each class are called back to compete for Best of Breed rather than separate sex prizes. If the show is not judged on the group system then every best of breed winner will compete together for the award of Best in Show. The same competition will then be judged for Best Puppy in Show.

You will find that at local open shows you will bump into people from your training class and there is more of a small community air to the occasion. The smaller open shows will not have so many trade stands in attendance so make sure that you have all your equipment with you as it may be hard to purchase a new show lead or a bottle of your favourite cleaning fluid.

GROUP JUDGING

Some shows are judged on the group system, which means that every dog in the working group who won best of breed will compete for one of four group placings. There is often judging for puppy groups as well. These details will be shown in your schedule and catalogue. Each winner of the seven groups then competes for Best in Show, followed by the judging for Best Puppy in Show.

To even win a place at your very first show is a big achievement and an honour not gained by many at the beginning of their show career. But, win or lose, after your first day at a dog show you will certainly have been bitten by the dog showing bug.

ITEMS TO PACK FOR THE SHOW

- Water
- Bowl for water and food
- A spray plant mister
- Kitchen paper
- Corn or potato flour
- Bench chain
- Boots and coat for dog
- Wet wipes – canine and human
- Brush
- Comb
- Show lead
- Ring clip
- Passes to get into the show
- Small first aid kit for yourself
- First aid kit for your dog
- Plenty of plastic bags to pick up after your dog
- Rescue remedy
- A good map
- Mobile phone
- Clean trousers
- Drinks for yourself
- Food for handler
- Food for dog
- Treats for your dog – win or lose

Author's story

We all have our favourite dog shows and one of mine is the Windsor Championship show held each summer in Windsor Home Park with the castle in the background. Always attending on pastoral day we often wonder if Her Majesty The Queen will pop down to watch the Corgis being judged – we live in hope. Windsor was the first general championship show that we entered in 1973. Such was the size of our breed in those days that we were in the minor puppy bitch class with about 30 other puppies. The judge back then was a young Mrs Ann Davis (Now Mrs Ann Arch) and she picked our Holly to be in the final cut of ten in the class. We were not placed but were so thrilled and of course like many others we were hooked on the dog show world. I can still see the showground, the old fashioned marquees and the friendly faces of exhibitors now long gone – happy days.

Another showground that I love to visit is the Three Counties showground at Malvern. We often stayed over and made a visit to a show into a weekend. Warm evenings sitting by the river Severn, pint in hand and talking about dogs to all who stopped to admire our brood – everyone should try this. Our dogs loved to stay in small guesthouses and were generally looked after and spoilt by the owners.

A good exhibitor...

Enjoys their first shows and doesn't worry about winning a place or qualifying for Crufts.

A bad exhibitor...

Arrives late and leaves early, never congratulates the class winner and generally complains about the show.

7

Rules and Etiquette

For a beginner in dog showing the rules surrounding the sport will seem mind-boggling. As you progress with your new hobby you will realise that most of the rules are needed for the world of dogs, including the show section, to run as smoothly as possible.

THE RED BOOK

Originally the Kennel Club started for a group of dog enthusiasts and, like any club, they needed a few rules to follow. Over the years and with the growth of the dog fancy, the rule book has grown and grown until today when it encompasses every part of the canine world, from club membership to dog show rules.

The Kennel Club publishes the rule book yearly. As new rules are made or old ones changed by the various sub-committees they are included in the monthly *Kennel Gazette* publication, which is also worth reading as it gives an insight into the world of the pedigree dog. Although the rule book goes by the grand name of *Kennel Club Rules and Regulations*, within the committees, show goers and Kennel Club members it is known as 'the red book' due to the colour of its cover.

The book includes a list of the members of the Kennel Club as well as all the breed clubs and training clubs that are affiliated to the Kennel Club. Members of the Kennel Club receive a copy, as does each secretary of the affiliated clubs as they are expected to follow the rules and use the book for reference. If you ever need to contact breed club secretaries or look for training classes in your area, the red book is the place to look although these days the Kennel Club website covers much of the information you are likely to need.

Breaking a Rule

Showing your dog may be a hobby but break a rule and you are penalised. It could be something as small as entering the wrong class or putting the wrong sire's name on your show entry form, but it could lead you to lose an award that has taken time to prepare for and hard work to win.

It is worth making sure that your show entries are completed correctly before you seal the envelope or push the send button on your computer. Some people use their computer to produce small sticky labels including details such as the dog's registered name, date of birth, dam, sire and so on, so they can peeled off and stuck straight onto the entry form. Some of the printing companies that provide a show printing service keep a data file and if you are logged into this your dog's details are automatically printed onto the entry form.

Any awards that are taken from exhibitors are listed in the *Kennel Gazette*.

Making a Complaint

There may come a time when you see someone break a rule at a show or perhaps mistreat their dog. Sadly, there are a minority of people in every sport who try to cheat the system irrespective of their fellow competitors. If you feel strongly about what you have observed you can find the show secretary who will guide you through the complaint process. You will have to supply a statement and also name witnesses to the incident. If the incident is very serious the show management will call the local police for assistance. Don't be surprised if exhibitors who definitely witnessed an incident refuse to help you – many turn a blind eye in case it affects their dogs in future competition. Never approach the miscreant or try to admonish them yourself as you could become injured if tempers rise.

The show secretary will have to complete all the paperwork and file it with the Kennel Club for further consideration. Once paperwork is processed at the Kennel Club they will decide whether to call the guilty party before the disciplinary sub-committee for a hearing. Depending on the severity of the case, the parties involved may have witnesses called and hire the representation of lawyers.

The outcome of a disciplinary hearing can mean simply a fine or being banned from breeding, exhibiting – even entering the vicinity of a showground for a number of years. You can see that a ban of this magnitude can affect the whole future of someone who is deeply involved in their breed. The Kennel Club never takes lightly any exhibitor that brings the world of dogs into disrepute.

THINKING OF OTHERS

When you set out on your new hobby always be considerate of fellow exhibitors. If you have a bitch and she comes into season, leave her at home. Not only will she not be at her best at this time but you can disrupt hundreds of dogs at the show and cause mayhem. Handling a dog in the ring after an in season bitch has stood there is hell. All he wants to do is sniff the ground and mark the territory. Some male dogs will even become short tempered with other dogs in the show ring, which can be quite dangerous. Even wiping your bitch clean and using sprays will not dampen the ardour of a determined dog.

A tip for stopping your dog from sniffing the ground for a bitch's scent is to rub a little of your own perfume or aftershave on your dog's chest. If he can only smell your odour he may settle down.

IN THE RING

When in the show ring try not to stack your dog close to the next dog as it can be off putting.

When moving your dog never run into fellow exhibits or try to put off their dogs from moving correctly. This can happen and is very bad sportsmanship. If you know that certain exhibitors are over zealous in their show techniques, keep away from them when you next meet in the ring.

When setting up your dog never step forward so that the judge gains a better view of your dog. If we all did this we would end up in a huddle in the centre of the show ring!

BEING FIRST

Some people make a habit of wanting to race into the ring as soon as the class is called to bag the first place in the line up of dogs for exhibition. This smacks of being over keen and, besides, the judge can decide to move the line up or judge them numerically. When waiting to enter the ring never block the entrance as it holds up proceedings and annoys exhibitors. You will start to recognise the people who want to be first and dominate the ring. Don't worry about them; the judge is there to give every dog his few minutes in the spotlight regardless of where in the line up you stand.

ARRIVING LATE

Try to be ringside when your class is called. Although the ring steward will call out once the names of any missing exhibitors before handing the ring to the judge for assessment, it is poor show to run into the ring after judging has begun. Some judges are lenient and will allow you to tack onto the end of the line up – but many won't and you would have made an expensive entry and a long journey for nothing.

Sometimes there are hold ups on the motorways and show starting times are delayed to accommodate the many exhibitors arriving late. If you find that you have missed your first class you will still be allowed to exhibit in the other classes that you have entered.

MAKING ENEMIES

Sadly some people can take a disliking to you in the show world when you have never even spoken to them. It could be jealousy of your lovely puppy or even that they have noted who bred your dog and have issues with them. At times, exhibiting can be very strange and we can wonder why we even go to some shows. Simply smile and speak to the friendly people – never give the nasty ones ammunition or you have an enemy for life. There are more nice people in the dog show world than nasty ones but at times it feels like the opposite!

THE JUDGE

Whatever you think of your judge smile nicely and leave the ring. Do not question their judgement or speak to them. They have a job to do and cannot stop to justify their choice of prize winners to every exhibitor. Never stand outside the ring and discuss the judge's parentage. If you are upset or angry get into your car and go home.

Unless the judge has blatantly done something wrong – in which case lodge a complaint with the show secretary – show your disapproval by voting with your feet. In other words, never give this judge an entry again. When enough people feel unhappy with a bad judge they will lose entries and not be invited to judge much more. This is because show societies need entries to make a profit and pay for the show.

You could also write to your breed club and explain your problem with the judge, as each club keeps their own list of people that they approve of to undertake judging appointments. If there is enough evidence, when the judges' list is next discussed the breed club committee will consider whether to exclude this person from their list.

BENCHING AREA

There never seems to be enough room on the benches, whether you are showing a Great Dane or a West Highland White Terrier. With grooming tables, blankets, bags and dogs it is easy to overspill into another person's territory. Try to keep within your allotted space, put your grooming table in the grooming area and make friends with your near neighbours – you are bound to meet again at other shows and it doesn't help if you are growling at each other for the next ten years.

The benching area is usually in a marquee at the outdoor shows and it can get very hot and noisy. If you find this is upsetting your dog try to find a quiet shaded area outside where you and your dog can sit and wait to go into the ring.

RESPECTING THE SHOW SECRETARY

Show secretaries are very busy and do not enjoy taking telephone calls at all hours asking about an entry or the time of judging. If you have a serious question try to use email and do not interrupt the secretary's time.

DEALING WITH DOG WASTE

Pick up after your dog at all times and bin the bag afterwards. Approaching large venues such as the National Exhibition Centre in Birmingham for Crufts, there is no worse sight than rows of poo bags or, worse still, dog waste walked into the pavements and the roads where owners just haven't bothered to clear up after their pet.

Try not to let your dog empty his bowels in the show ring. Take him for a walk before the class is called – he will feel more comfortable and you will not be embarrassed by being handed the poo bucket by the ring steward and having to shovel up the hot steaming deposit in front of a cheering crowd.

APPROACHING OTHER DOGS

There may be a dog or two that you would like to stroke when at a show. Always ask permission from the owner and always wait until after the dog has been in the ring. Not only will the owner be psyched up and ready to show, all their careful grooming may be spoilt and the dog could become excitable.

Always approach a dog from the head and never the rear end as he could become spooked and snappy – if he is so inclined.

DRESS CODE

Although there is not exactly a dress code for exhibitors, it goes without saying that you should be clean and presentable. If you have a long journey to the show carry a fresh shirt or top and a hair brush – or borrow the dog's one. You do your dog no service by looking unshaven or unkempt. For men, trousers that do not fall down and for women, skirts that are not too short or tops that are not too low make simple sense.

BAITING

Some people use small titbits of food to bait their dogs in the ring, making their dogs seem more alert to the judge. For some breeds this is frowned upon, while for others it is normal practise. Try not to be too free and easy with the bait as it can cause problems for dogs that follow after you into the show ring. If there is a scattering of chopped liver or small biscuits in the grass it is very hard to keep a dog's attention and expect him to perform for a judge.

Unentered dogs

If you have not entered a dog, leave him at home. Unentered dogs are not allowed to go into a showground. If you know that the dog will not have a sitter while you are at the show, enter him 'not for competition' and this way he will be allocated a bench and can be with you all day long. Some larger championship shows have a marquee just outside the show entrance where unentered dogs can be left for the day. The dogs are cared for by volunteers from local canine charities who just require a donation for this service.

Under no circumstances leave your dog in your car. Dogs die in the heat and, not only will you be prosecuted, you will have lost one of your beloved pets just for the chance to enter a show. If you have problems with care for your dog do not go to the show.

Groups

You may be fortunate and win a Best Puppy or a Best of Breed award. Always stay and compete in the group as it is so disappointing to your judge not to see the dogs they put up make an appearance. You are representing your breed and it is an honour to have won a place in the group, so enjoy the occasion. If for any reason you cannot stay for the group judging make a point of speaking to your breed judge and explain why you are leaving early. It is not normally your breed judge who presides in the group ring. You will have another judge, possibly someone well known in the dog show world, so try to stay and compete.

Be polite

Whatever your feelings at a show, congratulate fellow exhibitors and smile. Do not race off after your class but stay and cheer on the class winners as they compete for Best of Breed and remember to wish them luck in the group ring or Best in Show ring. If you see the judge after he or she has completed their duties, try to have a few words as this is when you will learn about your breed. In years to come it's so nice to look back and remember when one of the great names in your breed gave you advice at the beginning of your showing career.

Author's story

❛ *Serving on breed committees over the years, I've seen my fair share of paperwork. To be honest the majority of exhibitors, committee members and judges are honest and trustworthy, but just sometimes one finds a person ready to bend the rules or not follow them at all. My view has always been that if you want to serve on a committee it is not for what you can get from it but what you can do to help your breed or your show society. When I unearthed dodgy goings on by a fellow officer and a potential judge blurring the truth with their application to award challenge certificates, I was quick to find out that there were many fellow committee members prepared to leave well alone and not rock the boat. This is not the way to run a breed club; we love our breeds too much to see people bring them into possible disrepute.*

Remember, if you ever come across people breaking the rules of the sport that you hold dear never bury your head in the sand but stand proud and do your part in bringing the miscreants to hand.

Staying for the group judging is a lovely way to end the day at a dog show. Even if you have not won Best of Breed or Best Puppy, stay and cheer on fellow people in your breed and one day they may do the same for you. ❜

A good exhibitor...

Never breaks rules to win in competition. They care for their sport and will do whatever they can to see that the public respects the world of dogs.

A bad exhibitor...

Will win at all costs and not care about bad sportsmanship neither in the ring nor in the world of show dogs.

8

Awards and Prizes

Showing your dog is about winning, after all no one enters a competition wanting to lose do they? But as you progress with your new hobby you will find that any place you win in your class comes second to the enjoyment you receive from becoming part of a dog loving community. You will make many new friends from all walks of life and many parts of the world who, if it had not been for your dog, you would never have met in your normal life.

TROPHIES

When you enter a breed club's show you will see a vast array of trophies on the secretary's table. Take a few moments to look at the awards and read the inscriptions. Many trophies are named after famous kennels, dogs and people in your chosen breed and can be very old. Some trophies are inscribed with the winner's name, so if you are fortunate to win your class not only can you take the trophy home for one year but your name is added to the roll of honour for future generations to read.

The job of the trophy steward on the breed committee is a thankless task, as the trophies have to be stored, maintained and cleaned before every show. Not only that but the trophies that are taken by the winners at the previous show have to be collected and this is quite a time consuming job. Usually, in order to be able to take a trophy home after a show, you have to be a member of the club. A deposit will also be required to safeguard the return of what is a piece of club history. Sadly, many cups and trophies are lost by careless members and stories are often told of them turning up at boot fairs and jumble sales. If you ever spot a trophy that you think belongs with a dog show society, notify the club secretary who will be very pleased to see it back where it belongs.

ROSETTES

A table full of beautiful rosettes made from satin and ribbon is a sight to behold at every show and with luck you will be taking a few home with you. There is a colour code for the rosettes: first place is red, second is blue, third is yellow, fourth (which is called reserve) is green and fifth (which is called very highly commended) is often white or lilac. The centre of the rosette will bear the name of the show society or club and also the place won.

Apart from place wins, in each class there are rosettes for best puppy, best of breed, reserve best of breed through to top honours like best in show. So on a good day you can carry home a vast array of colourful rosettes. A pin board on a wall can display many rosettes and, put up in the right place, it will be seen by all visitors as a mark of success for your dog.

PLACE CARDS

Many show societies hand out place cards even if they cannot afford to give rosettes. Each card is coloured in the same way as the rosettes and displays the show details and the place number. By keeping these in a ringbinder you can look back on your dog's show career long after he has retired from the ring.

GOODIES

Dog shows are often sponsored by dog food companies or companies known to committee members. At a generous show you may win vouchers or sacks of dog food and other treats to take home with you. It is amazing what can be on offer at some shows, even money for top winners donated by club members which is a bonus when you have such an expensive hobby. Never think you will make a fortune from dog showing as even at Crufts the top winner will only go home with several hundred pounds after winning his way from breed class to Best in Show.

CHALLENGE CERTIFICATE

Challenge Certificates are won at championship shows when they are shown in the schedule as being on offer to your breed. Usually there is a set of CCs (as they are known): one for the Best Dog and one for the Best Bitch. When a dog has won three Challenge Certificates under three different judges, he is verified by the Kennel Club and declared a champion in the breed.

Sounds simple doesn't it? Don't you believe it! To win Best Dog or Best Bitch you first have to win your class. Next you have to go into the challenge against all the other unbeaten dogs of the same sex and be declared Best of Sex – then you win your Challenge Certificate. In numerically high breeds this means beating many hundreds of dogs. The Challenge Certificate has to be signed by the judge to make it official. In order to qualify as a champion one of the CCs must be won when the dog is over 12 months old.

A Reserve Challenge Certificate is also awarded to the runner up in each sex. This certificate states that if the Challenge Certificate is taken away from the winner for any reason the reserve winner is then given the award. This can and does happen.

Junior Warrant

If you have a young dog that is doing quite well, it is worth considering trying to collect enough points from show wins to qualify him for his Junior Warrant. By winning the Junior Warrant your dog will also be listed in the Kennel Club stud book, just as Challenge and Reserve Challenge Certificate winners are, and he can also have the letters JW after his name in show catalogues. It is a very special achievement to have your dog's name in the stud book and to be awarded a stud book number. Once a dog has a stud book number he has qualified for Crufts for life.

The Kennel Club guidelines for attaining the award are as follows:

- You must have 25 points in total: 3 points are awarded from each championship show win and 1 point is awarded for every open show win.

- You can only claim points if you are placed first in a breed class, such as puppy, graduate, limit, open, etc. Note that best puppy, any variety and any variety not separately classified classes do not count.

- The dog must be between 6 and 18 months of age when claiming points.

- A minimum of 3 points must be from championship shows.

- A minimum of 3 points must be from open shows.

- JW points cannot be claimed if there are less than three dogs present in the class.

■ You can claim 1 point for the Best of Breed award, but only if
   you were not able to claim a point for a first prize in a breed
   class and only when there are three or more dogs present in
   the breed.

■ You can claim points for 'special' breed classes, such as special
   beginners and special yearling, providing these classes are
   listed under the breed classification and the relevant numbers
   of dogs are present.

■ You can claim points for 'stakes' classes at a single breed show
   provided the relevant number of dogs are present.

You need to keep a detailed record of your show wins in order to
make your claim. The form for this claim is downloadable from the
Kennel Club website and some exhibitors find it useful to
download the form and add the wins as and when they are won.

SHOW CERTIFICATE OF MERIT

This award is relatively new. It came into effect 1 January 2003 and
was brought about to try and boost the number of people attending
general open shows. It is now a valued qualification and something
to achieve if you do not have your sights set on higher honours.
Once awarded, ShCM may be included after the dog's name.

The award is achieved by winning points at shows as follows:

■ 25 points in total can be claimed from placings at general open
   shows or group open shows.

■ 5 points must be won in Group Competition.

■ 5 points for Best in Show.

- 4 points for Single Group Best in Show.

- 3 points for Reserve Best in Show at a general open show or group open show not judged on the group system. Effective 1 February 2006.

- Points are given for multi-group placings (note that puppy group placings do not count): 4 points for first, 3 points for second, 2 points for third, 1 point for fourth.

- 1 point for Best Any Variety Not Separately Classified (AVNSC) (that is, AVNSC Hound, AVNSC Gundog, winner of overall Best AVNSC).

- 1 point for Best of Breed.

BREEDER'S COMPETITION

A major competition launched in 2009 is the Kennel Club Breeder's Competition. Breeders are able to compete with each other to demonstrate their breeding skills and to show off their stock.

There will be a Crufts Final in 2010 with the following main features:

- Competitions are scheduled at all championship shows for every breed, with or without CCs (breed club, sub group, group and general championship shows included).

- Entries can be made on the day of the competition.

- Breeders become eligible to enter by having bred four dogs that are present and exhibited at that show in that breed.

- The competition is judged by the breed judge immediately after awarding Best of Breed and Best Puppy in Breed.

- Best Breeder in Breed goes through to a Best Breeder in Group award.

A cumulative points system will be applied to all wins:

- 20 points are available per calendar year: 1 point for a breed win, 4 points for winning a group, 3 points for coming second in a group, 2 points for third place in a group, 1 point for fourth place in a group.

- After achieving 20 points in a calendar year, breeders withdraw from competition for the rest of that year.

- 20 points are required to qualify for the semi final or final at Crufts in the following year. (The total number of qualifiers may dictate that additional heats or qualifications are necessary to secure a place in the final.)

A breeder's competition record is available from the Kennel Club.

DOG OF THE YEAR

'Of the year' competitions pop up quite often, either within your own breed or through local canine societies. Breed club dog of the year competitions are quite prestigious affairs and invitations are usually sent to the dogs that have made major wins during the past 12 months. There is usually a formal dinner, with everyone wearing their posh frocks, before invited secret judges assess the dogs and hand over awards. These occasions are ideal for meeting fellow exhibitors and followers of your breed without the stresses of the showground to contend with – unless your dog is competing of course!

Regional competitions are organised on a similar basis such as Kent Dog of the Year or Welsh Dog of the Year. The dogs are usually Best in Show or Best Puppy in Show winners from designated shows held in the area. Sometimes there is a proviso that the exhibitor must live in the area covered, other times the qualification is more flexible.

These types of events are covered by the canine and local press and are a very prestigious item to have listed on your showing CV.

STAKES CLASS

Most dog shows schedule stakes classes, some just as an extra class with the prize awarded on the day of the show. At some major championship shows the winner of the stakes class will return to compete against other winners from each day of the show. The overall winner goes on to compete at the end of the year for the title Pup of the Year or perhaps Junior of the Year.

These competitions are sponsored by major canine food companies or perhaps a pet insurance company and the number of entries can be very high. There is a lot of publicity surrounding these competitions and the prizes can be quite substantial. Take a look at the next show schedule you receive and read about the stakes classes – some are even named after well-known people once associated with the show society with the funds from the entry money being donated to a charity.

Remember that you will already be at the show so another entry will not be too expensive.

TRAINING CLUB AWARDS

Another popular award is normally found closer to home. Your ringcraft classes will quite often have a points system where you log your class wins throughout the year by showing your prize cards, and prizes are awarded at the annual Christmas party. These events are great fun with games for owners and dogs and a visit from Santa. Many dogs don fancy dress, leading to much hilarity.

Author's story

❨ *We once entered a dog show while on holiday in Cornwall. Our lovely puppy Oliver won his class and was declared Best Puppy in Breed. We took home the large wooden shield, which was covered with small silver shields with the names of winning puppies from years gone by. The following year we had to return the trophy but were not planning a holiday in the West Country. With the engraving costs and secure postage back to the trophy steward, that one win cost us a lot of money. After that we simply carried a camera to the shows and if we won a trophy we photographed the dog and his award and left the trophy with the club for safe keeping.*

Campaigning a dog for an award such as a Junior Warrant can be costly and very tiring for both handler and dog. Remember that your dog is still quite young and to take him to every show going just to boost your points is doing him no favours. We have witnessed on several occasions the stress of reaching the target points for owners and consequently dogs. Once when we beat a dog to second place and won a Junior Warrant, it was almost war as the lady owner who came second was so angry as she had lost her last chance to win a point for her own dog. If you feel you could not cope under this competitiveness then do not enter these competitions.

A good exhibitor...

Will return trophies on time and keep them safe and clean. Will always consider their dog when competing for points for awards. They will not tire the dog by constantly pushing to win at any cost.

A bad exhibitor...

Often lets down their breed club by not returning a trophy and disappointing the next person who wins the award.

Will race around the country with no thought for their dog's stress levels or health as they maniacally collect point after point to win competitions.

9

Major Championship Shows

As you begin your journey into the world of dog showing, you will find that not a week goes by without there being a dog show within driving distance of your home. Some shows will be fun companion shows organised to raise funds for worthwhile causes. Other shows will be organised by breed clubs and only open to dogs of that particular breed – you may not own that particular breed of dog but it can still be an enjoyable and educational day if you choose to attend. The format of the show will be the same as any other show and the owners love their dogs just as much as you love yours.

You may see advertisements for group shows at both open and championship level which, again, you may not be able to enter but they are great fun to attend as a spectator. Remember, we dog show folk never stop learning about dogs! There are also general shows held every week, which can be open shows meaning they are open for all breeds to enter.

The major general championship shows are well known amongst exhibitors and, apart from a few adjustments due to weather and diary changes, they occur each year around the same time. Many exhibitors plan their holidays around the major shows. With so many scheduled within weeks of each other during the summer months, it is possible to attend around six during your summer vacation.

CRUFTS

The major show in all exhibitors' diaries is Crufts. Held over four days each March, this is the only show in the United Kingdom that entrants need to have qualified for in order to enter. Organised by the Kennel Club from their headquarters in Clarges Street, Piccadilly, London, this show attracts around 20,000 entries from around the world and has a gate of 125,000 people. Although all shows are open to the public, it is Crufts that attracts the general public in droves to see all that is great about dogs and their owners. Currently staged at the National Exhibition Centre in Birmingham, come the first week in March all roads lead to the Midlands for the greatest dog show on earth!

Qualifying to enter a dog for Crufts is based on wins gained during the previous year. The introduction of the pet passport opened doors for dogs from around the world to enter. Entry requirements differ from country to country and are regularly updated on the Crufts' website. Below are the entry requirements needed for Crufts 2009.

Crufts 2009 qualifications for entry of dogs

Source: www.thekennelclub.org.uk

1. A DOG UNDER 8 CALENDAR MONTHS OF AGE ON THE 5 MARCH 2009 IS NOT ELIGIBLE FOR ENTRY AT THIS SHOW UNLESS IT HAS QUALIFIED FOR ENTRY IN THE KENNEL CLUB STUD BOOK. N.B. A puppy so qualified which is between 6 and 8 months of age is not eligible for entry in Special Puppy or Special Junior.

2. THE FOLLOWING ARE THE QUALIFICATIONS A DOG MUST HAVE FOR ENTRY AT CRUFTS 2009.

a) Entry in breed classes at Crufts 2009, where Challenge Certificates are offered.

A dog is eligible for entry in breed classes where Challenge Certificates are offered if it has qualified in any of the following ways under the Rules and Regulations of the Kennel Club.

1.   If it is a Champion, Show Champion, Field Trial Champion, Working Trial Champion, Obedience Champion or Agility Champion under the Rules of the Kennel Club.

2.   If it is entered in the Kennel Club Stud Book, or qualifies for entry in the Kennel Club Stud Book by 5 January 2009.

3.   If it is entered in the Kennel Club Stud Book, or qualifies for entry in the Kennel Club Stud Book by 5 January 2009 through Field Trials or Working Trials.

4.   If it has won any of the following prizes in a breed class (as defined in Kennel Club Regulations for the Definitions of Classes at Championship Shows) at a Championship Show, including Crufts, where Challenge Certificates were offered for the breed between 7 January 2008 and 5 January 2009.
      i.   First, Second or Third in Minor Puppy Class
      ii.   First, Second or Third in Puppy Class
      iii.   First, Second or Third in Junior Class
      iv.   First, Second or Third in Yearling Class (for Breeds in Stud Book Band E only – see list below)
      v.   First, Second or Third in Post Graduate Class
      vi.   First, Second or Third in Limit Class
      vii.   First, Second or Third in Open Class
      viii. First, Second or Third in Veteran Class

Stud Book Band E

Hound Group – Whippet

Gundog Group – Irish Setter, Retriever (Flat Coated), Retriever (Golden), Retriever (Labrador), Spaniel

(Cocker)

Terrier Group – Border Terrier, Staffordshire Bull Terrier

Utility Group –

Pastoral Group – Bearded Collie, Border Collie, Shetland Sheepdog

Working Group – Boxer, Dobermann, Great Dane, Rottweiler

Toy Group – Cavalier King Charles Spaniel

5. If it has won a first prize in *any* breed class at Crufts 2008. (NB *This is in addition to those dogs which have qualified in classes listed under 2a (4) above.*)

6. If a Beagle, has won a First Prize at a Hound Show between 7 January 2008 and 5 January 2009 held under the Rules and Regulations of the Masters of Harriers and Beagles Association.

7. Premier Open Show
For dogs that have been declared Best of Breed provided there were more than three breed classes (*more than five classes for Stud Book Band E breeds*) scheduled for the breed between 7 January 2008 and 5 January 2009.

8. If it has won Best in Show, Reserve Best in Show or Best Puppy in Show at a General or Group Open Show between 7 January 2008 and 5 January 2009.

b) Entry in breed classes at Crufts 2009 for Bracco Italiano, Dogue de Bordeaux, Portuguese Podengo and Spanish Water Dog and where challenge certificates are not offered.

A dog is eligible for entry in breed classes where Challenge Certificates are not offered if it has qualified in any of the following ways under the Rules and Regulations of the Kennel Club.

1. If it has been declared Best of Sex or Reserve Best of Sex of a Breed or gained any of the following prizes in Breed or Variety Classes at a Championship Show, including Crufts between 7 January 2008 and 5 January 2009.

    i.   First, Second or Third in Minor Puppy Class

    ii.   First, Second or Third in Puppy Class

    iii. First, Second or Third in Junior Class

    iv. First, Second or Third in Post Graduate Class

    v.   First, Second or Third in Limit Class

    vi. First, Second or Third in Open Class

    vii. First, Second or Third in Veteran Class

    (See note 2.)

2.   If it has won a first prize in *any* breed class at Crufts 2008. (N.B. *This is in addition to those dogs which have qualified in classes listed under 2b (1) above.*)

3.   Premier Open Show
For dogs that have been declared Best of Breed provided there were more than three breed classes (*more than five classes for Stud Book Band E breeds*) scheduled for the breed.

4.   If it has won Best in Show, Reserve Best in Show or Best Puppy in Show at a General or Group Open Show held between 7 January 2008 and 5 January 2009.

c) Entry in Field Trial classes at Crufts 2009.
A dog is eligible for entry in Field Trial classes for its breed if it has at any time won an award, a Diploma of Merit or a Certificate of Merit in actual competition at a Field Trial held under Kennel Club or Irish Kennel Club Regulations.

d) Entry in Special Working Gundog classes at Crufts 2009.
A dog is eligible for entry in Special Working Gundog classes for its breed if it has at any time been awarded a Working Gundog Certificate, a Kennel Club Show Gundog Working Certificate or won an award, Diploma of Merit or Certificate of Merit in competition at a Field Trial held under the rules of any governing body recognised by the Kennel Club

e) Entry in Special Working Trial classes at Crufts 2009.
With the exception of Bloodhounds, a dog is eligible for entry in

Working Trial classes for its breed if it has gained a qualification not lower than UD Excellent under Kennel Club Working Trial Regulations. A Bloodhound is eligible for entry in Working Trial classes if it has won a prize at a Working Trial for Bloodhounds held under Kennel Club Working Trial Regulations.

f) Obedience Championships at Crufts 2009.
A dog is eligible for entry if it has won a Kennel Club Obedience Certificate at a Show held between 7 January 2008 and 5 January 2009.

g) Agility Championships at Crufts 2009.
A dog is eligible for entry if it has won a Kennel Club Agility Certificate (Large, Medium and Small Dogs) at a show held between 7 January 2008 and 5 January 2009.

h) Qualified dogs too young to compete in 2008.
A dog which gained a qualifying award prior to 7 January 2008 but was under 8 months of age on 6 March 2008 and, therefore, ineligible for competition at Crufts 2008, is eligible for Crufts 2009 without further qualification.

i) Overseas qualifications.
The following qualifications refer to Kennel Club fully recognised breeds only.

1. Any Champion from a country with which the Kennel Club has a reciprocal agreement qualifies automatically if it is domiciled in the UK and is on the Kennel Club Breed Register.

2. Any FCI International Beauty Champion.

3. Winners of Junior Dog and Junior Bitch classes, plus the Best Dog and the Best Bitch at specified shows in each of the European countries entitled to take part in the UK Pets Travel Scheme. One show only nominated by the Kennel Club in the country concerned.

4.   Winners of Junior Dog, Junior Bitch classes, plus CACIB Dog and CACIB Bitch at FCI World Winners Show 2008. Winners of Junior Dog, Junior Bitch, Veteran Dog, Veteran Bitch plus CACIB Dog and CACIB Bitch at European Winners Shows in 2008. This applies to dogs resident in countries entitled to take part in the UK Pets Travel Scheme.

5.   **USA** – Winners of Best of Breed, Best of Opposite, Awards of Merit and Best Bred by Exhibitor in the classes at the AKC Invitational, December 2008. Additionally, Best of Breed, Best of Opposite, Awards of Merit Winners (if offered) and Best Bred by Exhibitor (if offered), at one National Breed Speciality show per breed chosen by the Parent Breed Club and agreed by the AKC.

6.   **Canada** – The top five dogs from each group according to the *Dogs in Canada* Top Show Dog point system, published in *Dogs in Canada* July issue. Additionally, Best of Breed, Best of Opposite and Award of Merit Winners at the National Specialities agreed by the Canadian Kennel Club.

7.   **Australia** – One Show has/will be nominated for 2008 in each of the eight states. Winners of Junior Dog and Junior Bitch classes, plus the Best Dog and the Best Bitch to qualify at each show.

Location	Name of Show
Australian Capital Territory (ACTCA)	Canberra Royal Championship Dog Show
Western Australia (CAWA)	Advance Western Classic
Queensland (CCCQ)	Brisbane Royal Show
Northern Territory (NACA)	Royal Darwin Show
New South Wales (DOGS NSW)	Spring Fair Dog Show (Sunday only)
South Australia (SACA)	Advance Autumn International Championship Show (Sunday only)
Tasmania (TCA)	Royal Hobart Show
Victoria (VCA)	Melbourne Royal Show

8. **Japan** – Winners of Best King and Best Queen also Best Junior King and Best Junior Queen at FCI Asian International Championship Show 2008, Tokyo.

9. **New Zealand** – Winners of Junior Dog and Junior Bitch classes, plus the Best Dog and Best Bitch to qualify from the NZKC ProPlan National Show.

10. **Ireland** – Winners of Junior Dog and Junior Bitch plus Best Adult Dog and Best Adult Bitch from the seven Irish Kennel Club Group Championship Shows.

Notes on qualifications

1. A Breed Class is a class confined to one breed.

2. Awards as above qualify a dog for entry at Crufts 2009 only if the class in which the award was gained was not made 'Special' in any way, i.e. by age, colour, height, weight, coat, to members of a society, to breeders, etc. An exception is made only in the case of prize winners in Special Puppy, Special Junior and Veteran at Crufts 2008. Wins in sweepstake classes do not qualify nor do wins in any classes other than those stated above.

3. Only dogs of 8 calendar months of age or over on 5 March 2009 will be eligible for entry at Crufts 2009 unless a Kennel Club Stud Book qualification has been obtained.

4. In any class scheduled at Crufts 2009 for which an age limit appears in the definition, the age is calculated to the 5 March 2009.

5. No entries will be accepted 'Not for Competition'.

Competing with docked or cropped dogs in the UK

*   **Docked dogs**

    Dogs which were docked before 6 April 2007 (28 March for shows held in Wales):

        If your dog was docked either in the UK or in a foreign country before 6 April 2007 (28 March for shows in

Wales) then it may compete at all Kennel Club licensed events.

Dogs which were docked on or after 6 April 2007 (28 March for shows held in Wales):

If your dog was docked on or after 6 April 2007 (28 March for shows held in Wales and irrespective of where it was docked) it will not, under the law, be permitted to be shown at any show in England or Wales where the public are admitted on payment of a fee.

However, if your dog was legally docked either in the UK or in another country *on or after* 28 March/6 April 2007, you will be permitted to compete with it at:

1.   all shows held in Scotland
2.   all shows held in Northern Ireland
3.   those shows held in England and Wales where the public do not pay to be admitted.

Shows where the public are admitted on payment of a fee:

All shows which charge the public for admission must state this on the show schedule and entry form – but you should check carefully whether or not your dog is eligible before entering.

• **Cropping**

No dog with cropped ears is eligible to compete at any Kennel Club licensed event.

As you can see, it can be quite confusing when you first consider trying to qualify for Crufts. Rather than reading through pages of rules and regulations, speak to fellow exhibitors in your breed as to which classes are qualifiers. If you are still unsure ring the Kennel Club for verification.

SHOWS

Show	Month	Day	Group
Boston & District Canine Society, Newark Mrs P.M. Dufty, Triken Watergate, Quadring Eaudyke, Spalding, Lincs, PE11 4PZ Tel: 01775 840295 Email: triken@btinternet.com	January	8 9 10	Gundog Hound/Pastoral/ Working Utility/Toy/Terrier
Manchester Dog Show Society, Staffordshire Mr P. Harding, Pringham House, 324 Warrington Road, Rainhill, Merseyside L35 9JA Tel: 0151 4267737/0779 3285628 Email: pringham@bulldogsuk. freeserve.co.uk	January	21 22 23 24	Terrier/Hound Utility/Toy Working/Pastoral Gundog
Crufts, N.E.C. Birmingham c/o Kennel Club, 1–5 Clarges Street, Piccadilly, London W1J 8AB Tel: 0870 6066750 Email: www.crufts.org.uk	March	11 12 13 14	Working/Pastoral Terrier/Hound/OB Toy/Utility/OB Gundog
Scottish Breeds Canine Club, Edinburgh Mr J. McCreath, 12 Motehill Road, Girvan, Ayrshire KA26 0EE Tel: 01465 714919 Email: scottishbreeds@aol.com	March	27	
United Kingdom Toy Dog Society, Stafford Mr T. Mather, 70 Higher Road, Hunts Cross, Liverpool L26 1TD Tel: 0151 4863570 Email: uktoydog@btinternet.com	March	27	

Show	Month	Day	Group
National Terrier Club, Stafford Mrs J. Griffiths, Home Farmhouse Cottage, Cardington Rd, Leebotwood, Shropshire SY6 6LX Tel: 01694 751258 Email: www.nationalterrier.co.uk	April	3	
Hound Association of Scotland, Kelso Mr A. Littlejohn, 15 Milton Drive, Kilmarnock, Ayrshire KA3 7HZ Tel: 01563 540194 Email: arcuilean@btinternet.com	April	10	
Working & Pastoral Breeds Association of Wales, Builth Wells Mrs J. Rual, Gilcoru Boarding Kennels, Waunlai Cottage, Tonyrefail, Mid Glam CF39 8YS Tel: 01443 672 089	April	17	
West of England Ladies Kennel Society, Malvern Mrs S. Jakeman, Lyneham Lake, Kingham, Chipping Norton, Oxon OX7 6UJ Tel: 01608 659369	April	23 24 25	Gundog/Toy Utility/Pastoral Hound/Working/Terrier
Birmingham Dog Show Society, Stafford Mr M. Townsend, Hawthorns, Oakley Road, Cheltenham, Gloucestershire GL52 6NZ Tel: 07866 159690 Email: townsend@waitrose.com	May	6 7 8 9	Utility/Toy Hound/Terrier Gundog Working/Pastoral

Show	Month	Day	Group
Scottish Kennel Club, Edinburgh Ms M. Orr, Paterson House, Eskmills Park, Station Road, Musselburgh EH21 7PQ Tel: 0131 665 3920	May	21 22 23	Working/Pastoral Gundog/Utility/OB Hound/Terrier/Toy/ AG
Bath Canine Society, Bath Mr K. Nathan, Chaworth Lodge, Annesley, Nottingham NG15 0AS Tel: 01623 754450 Email: bathcanine@aol.com	May	28 29 30 31	Terrier/Toy Gundog Working/Pastoral Hound/Utility
Southern Counties Canine Association, Newbury Mrs A. Cavill, Kingston House, Hilperton Road, Trowbridge, Wiltshire BA14 7JB Tel: 07905 162190 Email: Scca@angelacavill.co.uk Website: www.southerncounties dogshow.co.uk	June	4 5 6	Hound/Terrier/Toy Gundog/Utility Working/Pastoral
Three Counties Agricultural Society, Malvern Mrs J. Lane, Maythorn, Little Hereford, Ludlow, Shropshire SY8 4LJ Tel: 01584 711094 Email: lane@littlehereford. fsnet.co.uk	June	14 15 16 17	Pastoral/Terrier Utility/Hound Gundog Working/Toy
Border Union Agricultural Society, Kelso Mr B Stevenson, The Lodge Cottage, Carnham, Cornhill On Tweed, Coldstream TD12 4RW. Tel. No: 01890 830320 Email: dogs@border-union. freeserve.co.uk	June	19 20	Working/Pastoral/ Utility/Toy Gundog/Hound/ Terrier

Show	Month	Day	Group
Blackpool & District Canine Society, Blackpool Mr S. Hall, 'Shenedene', Gregson Lane, Hoghton, Preston, Lancashire PR7 0DP. Tel: 01254 853526 Email: secretary@blackpool dogshow.plus.com	June	25 26 27	Terrier/Utility/Toy Hound/Gundog Working/Pastoral
Windsor Dog Show Society, Windsor Mrs I. Terry, 13 Rennets Close, Eltham, London SE9 2NQ Tel: 020 8850 5321	July	1 2 3 4	Hound/Toy Terrier/Utility Working/Pastoral Gundog
East of England Agricultural Society, Peterborough Mrs J. M. Broadberry, East of England Showground, Peterborough PE2 6XE Tel: 01733 234451 Email: info@eastofengland. org.uk Website: www.eastofengland.org.uk	July	9 10 11	Working/Pastoral Hound/Toy/Terrier Gundog/Utility
National Working & Pastoral Breeds Dog Society, Malvern. Mrs A. Arch, The Corner House, 722 Walmersley Road, Bury, Lancs BL9 6RN Tel: 0161 762 9390	July	17	
Leeds City & District Canine Association, Harewood House Mrs E. Stannard, Summerhill, Sutton, Macclesfield, Cheshire SK11 0JD Tel: 01260 252834	July	24 25 26	Utility/Toy/Terrier Hound/Gundog Working/Pastoral

Show	Month	Day	Group
Hound Association, Stafford Mrs S. Rawlings, 31 Davenport Park, Gibralter Rise, Heathfield, Sussex TN21 8LE Tel: 01435 868908	August	7	
National Gundog Association, Malvern Mr C. Bexon, 59 Derby Road, Kirkby in Ashfield, Notts NG17 9DH Tel: 01623 722037 Email: Chris.bexon@fsmail.net	August	7	
Paignton & District Fanciers Association, Clyst, Devon Mrs A. Hodsoll, 32 Dart Bridge Road, Buckfastleigh, Devon TQ11 0DZ Tel: 01364 642420	August	2 3 4	Working/Pastoral Hound/Toy/Terrier Gundog/Utility
Bournemouth Canine Association, Brockenhurst Mrs D. Courtney, Foxholes Cottage, Poole Road, Sturminster Marshall, Wimborne, Dorset BH21 3RR Tel: 01258 857721	August	14 15 16	Terrier/Working/ Pastoral Utility/Gundog Hound/Toy
Welsh Kennel Club, Builth Wells Mr & Mrs G. Hill, Rose Cottage, West St, Llantwit Major, Vale of Glamorgan CF61 1SP Tel: 01446 792457	August	20 21 22	Hound/Toy Terrier/Working/ Pastoral/OB Gundog/Utility

Show	Month	Day	Group
Scottish Kennel Club, Edinburgh Ms M. Orr, Paterson House, Eskmills Park, Station Road, Musselburgh EH21 7PQ Tel: 0131 665 3920	August	28 29	Gundog/Terrier/ Hound Working/Pastoral/ Utility/Toy
City of Birmingham Canine Association, Warwickshire Mr K. Young, 17 Riversleigh Road, Leamington Spa, Warwicks CV32 6BG Tel: 01926 336 480	September	3 4 5	Hound/Toy Working/Pastoral/ Terrier Gundog/Utility
Richmond Dog Show Society, Surrey Dr R. James, Holmeswood Main Street, Old Weston, Cambs PE28 5LL Tel: 05602 318955 Email: secretary@richmonddog show.org.uk	September	10 11 12	Hound/Toy Working/Pastoral/ Terrier Gundog/Utility
Darlington Dog Show Society, Ripon Mrs F. N. Marshall, 'Gainspa', 1 Butler Road, Newton, Aycliffe, Co. Durham DL5 5LU Tel: 01325 312484 Email: darlingtonchampionship show@yahoo.com	September	17 18 19	Hound/Terrier/ Utility Working/Pastoral Gundog/Toy
Belfast Dog Show Society, Belfast Ms Brown, 47 Magheratimpany Road, Ballynahinch, Northern Ireland BT24 8NZ Tel: 028 9756 2716 Email: metkarcsp@aol.com	September	25 26	Hound/Gundog/ Terrier Utility/Working/ Pastoral/Toy

Show	Month	Day	Group
Driffield Agricultural Society, Wetherby Mr M.C. Freeman, Sunnyside, Long Lane, Shirebrook, Mansfield, Notts NG20 8AZ Tel. No: 01623 747006	September /October	30 1 2 3	Working/Pastoral Gundog Hound/Terrier Toy/Utility
South Wales Kennel Association, Buith Wells Mrs I.J. Dyke, 85 Ty-Glas Road, Llanishen, Cardiff CF4 5ED Tel: 029 20753584 Email: isobell.d@virgin.net	October	8 9 10	Toy/Hound/Terrier Gundog/Utility Pastoral/Working
Gundog Society of Wales, Malvern Mr R. Stafford, 193 Peniel Green Road, Llansamlet, Swansea, Wales SA7 9BA Tel: 01792 797404	October	13	
Midland Counties Canine Society, Stafford Mrs M.P. Everton, Ashram, Pickersleigh Road, Malvern Link, Malvern, Worcs WR14 2RS Tel: 01684 572375 Email: Margaret.Everton @onetel.com	October	28 29 30 31	Gundog Working/Terrier Toy/Utility Hound/Pastoral
Working & Pastoral Breeds Association of Scotland, Edinburgh Mrs S. Harkins, 15 Elizabeth Gardens, Stoneyburn, West Lothian EH47 8BP Tel: 07804 433226 Email: sheenaharkins@fsmail. net	November	6 7	Pastoral Working

Show	Month	Day	Group
Gundog Breeds Association of Scotland, Edinburgh Mr Haran, 2 Auchengree Road, Glengarnock, North Ayrshire, KA14 3BU Tel: 01505 685539 Email: gundogbreedscot @aol.com	November	13	
British Utility Breeds Association, Malvern Mrs M. Purnell-Carpenter, Overhill Kennels, Norton Lane, Pensford, Bristol BS39 4EY Tel: 01275 839560 Email: k9meg@overhill.co.uk	December	4	
Ladies Kennel Association, Birmingham Mrs L.F. Jupp, 60 Roundway, Camberley, Surrey GU15 1NU Tel: 01276 29495	December	11 12	Toy/Utility/ Working/Pastoral Hound/Gundog/ Terrier

As you can see, there are a lot of championship shows so there is bound to be a few near to your part of the country just in case you have no wish to spend your life travelling from show to show.

Do not forget that there are also your own breed championship shows to attend and they deserve your support as so much good work is undertaken by the committees and on a voluntary basis. Club fundraising, quite often undertaken at breed shows, is also valuable as much of it goes towards breed rescue.

On top of the championship shows there are also the multitude of open shows held every weekend of the year and most likely some will be very near to your home.

Obtaining schedules

Do not bother club secretaries for schedules until a few months before the shows as they will not have been printed and the secretary will be very busy organising the show along with fellow committee members. Check online to see if they are available to download. There are three main show printers and by checking their websites you can see all sorts of show information and also results:

- Higham Press Ltd: www.highampress.co.uk
- Fosse Data Systems: www.fossedata.com
- Canine Information Directory: www.canineinfo.idps.co.uk

Finding out who is judging

The judges picked for championship shows have to be passed by the Kennel Club show department several years before the actual show. The names of the judges are publicised regularly in the *Kennel Gazette*. By keeping up to date with the breed notes in the canine press you will hear who the judges are to be long before show schedules are printed. When new to showing you will be unaware of who the judges are and if they are breed specialists or all-rounders (who judge many breeds), so speaking to fellow exhibitors, your dog's breeder and keeping abreast of breed news in the post will give you a good idea of where to enter.

Keeping records

Remember to keep a record of your placings at championships shows including the class name and number just in case it is needed when applying for an award or to enter Crufts.

Author's story

❛ *The first time you qualify for Crufts is a magical moment. We had no idea that when we won third place in a large class with our puppy at the South Wales Championship Show that we had in fact qualified. Our dog's breeder and a friend were jumping around in excitement and, once we understood, we headed straight for the beer tent. I can still remember the day and still savour that extra special moment. We headed home on a high and never noticed the many hundreds of miles we covered as we were still so high on the achievement. Our puppy had no idea of his part in our celebrations and slept soundly.* ❜

A good exhibitor...

Will not bother the show secretary for a schedule but will download the paperwork well ahead of the show. The entry form will be completed correctly and sent off before the closing date.

A bad exhibitor...

Will expect the show secretary to post them a schedule and enter the show at the last moment without completing the form properly. They will not keep a record of their wins and will need to chase show secretaries for the information that they were neglectful in recording.

10

What Next?

You now have your dog and are exhibiting at shows both locally and around the UK. Have you noticed something? Your life is now starting to be planned around dog shows and training commitments. Next you will find that your dog-owning friends out number your 'non doggy' friends. You will be absent from family get-togethers as it's the weekend of the LKA championship show or another major event. The outfits you buy for your work's Christmas dinner dance is purchased more for its use in the ring at Crufts. Your holiday leave is spent at the summer shows or in a rented cottage so your dog can join the family.

I'm afraid it's bad news: you have the bug, the dog showing bug – and it's bitten big time! Life will never be the same.

So, what are you going to do next in your new hobby? Sure, it will be dog related but there are so many choices. You can read about these choices in canine publications such as *Dogs Monthly* and *Your Dog* or attend Crufts and Discover Dogs and watch owners and animals displaying their skills. The choice of canine pursuits is almost endless.

EXHIBIT OVERSEAS

If you enjoy competing in the UK perhaps you could try competition overseas. With the introduction of the Pet Travel

Scheme your dog can, once he has his pet passport, travel to many overseas countries where you can compete with fellow breed enthusiasts in their own countries.

Registering your dog for his own pet passport can take six months as he has to have rabies and other shots and then wait six months before blood tests are taken to ensure that they have worked. Your dog will also have to have been microchipped as he will be scanned during his travels.

Most veterinary surgeries now have facilities for customers who wish to travel with their dogs. You will also find that many fellow exhibitors that use the scheme to travel overseas will be able to allay any fears that you may have.

The checklist for the Pet Travel Scheme is:

- Microchip
- Rabies vaccinated
- Blood tests (after six months)
- Issue certification

Once you are travelling with your dog you will have to have him treated for tapeworm and ticks between 24 and 48 hours before he re-enters the UK. The rabies vaccinations need to be updated with booster injections so your dog can continue to travel.

BUY ANOTHER DOG

You have one dog that you enjoy exhibiting, so why not have a second? It may be that you are interested in another breed, in which case be as diligent with your research into suitable breeders as you were with your first dog. Take note that groups are often judged on different days so if your new breed is from another group you may find yourself split between which dog to show – or travelling twice to the same show.

If you wish to have a second dog from the same breed as your first you may just go back to the same breeder. Breeder loyalty is very common and if you were happy with your first dog it makes sense to continue with what you are happy with.

A second dog is very much like having a second child – you now have the experience of that first young life and know how to cope. You have much of the equipment and are not so fazed when small problems arise. Add to this your knowledge about training and the show world and you will find that life with a new puppy is easier second time around.

The added costs will be in purchases such as food and veterinary costs. Try to purchase pet insurance from a company that will give you a discount for having more than one dog – many will, but be prepared to haggle.

YOUR OWN KENNEL NAME

Have you noticed how some exhibitors have their own kennel name, called an affix? You will already have one in your own dog's name that belongs to his breeder. If you are serious about showing, and maybe one day want to breed a litter or two, then why not apply for your own affix? With an affix added to your dog's name you will become identified in catalogues and amongst your breed.

An affix can be added to the end of the name of any dog that you buy and when you breed it is at the front of the puppies' registered names. It is possible to download the application form from the Kennel Club and registration costs £70. Thereafter a maintenance fee of £20 (£17 by direct debit) is paid yearly.

BREEDING

After a few years of showing your dog you may decide to breed from her and have a litter. Never think that you can do this to make a profit as it is a fallacy that dog breeding is profitable. The only people to profit are puppy farmers and backyard breeders and you never want to go down that route!

Just as you studied your breed and planned your life around owning a dog, do the same when preparing for a litter of puppies. Attend seminars and read books, speak to breeders and ask questions until you are sure that breeding a litter is what you really want to do. Make sure that your bitch and the chosen stud dog has had every health check taken for the breed. If you are not sure about this then speak to the Kennel Club and also your breed club. Plan your time as you will need many free weeks to devote to the little ones and to your bitch. Having a litter of puppies is a most joyous time but must be planned with care.

BECOME A JUDGE

If judging interests you then perhaps, when you have enough experience under your belt, you could train to become a judge. In the interim years use your time to watch ringside and try to see why the judge favours some dogs over others. Speak to judges and learn from their comments. Attend seminars not only about judging but about the breeds that you are interested in, take the tests that are set and keep the certificates issued for attendance.

Eventually, when you are ready ask your breed club if you can be included on their C list of judges and wait to be invited to judge by a show committee. You are not able to judge your breed if your name is not on a breed club judging list.

Remember that not everyone is entitled to judge. It is an honour to be invited to assess your breed and it is not a given right.

JOIN A COMMITTEE

If you have the time to spare you could become part of your breed club committee or your local canine society committee. Although new committee members have to be voted on at the annual general meetings, it is not unknown for members to be co-opted during the year. To begin with you could just try helping out at the show, offering to help in the kitchen and clearing up afterwards is always welcome and when a committee vacancy occurs your name will be known to the members.

If your intention is to do committee work just so that you gain judges' appointments and further your show career, forget it! People like this are soon seen through and it will do more harm than good to your time in dogs. Sadly there are people like this on many committees and they hold back their breed but, over all, committees are made up of caring and loving members of the show world.

RESCUE WORK

Every breed club in the UK works to help their breed rescue, such as raising money to support less fortunate dogs and aid their upkeep. Other clubs actively collect dogs and find them new homes. These clubs are always in need of helpers and you too could be part of this. Why not start by fundraising for your breed rescue by organising a coffee morning, a raffle, a sponsored walk – it all helps those dogs less fortunate to find new 'furrever' homes.

PAT DOGS

Have you seen the dogs that visit hospitals to cheer up the patients? Pets As Therapy (PAT) dogs is an organisation devoted to helping others through contact with animals. As well as PAT dogs there are also PAT cats and PAT rabbits and the owners are trained to take their pets into care homes, children's wards, schools and many other places so that those who miss their pets can have a cuddle and remember their own pets. They also have schemes where children that have had bad encounters with animals can meet and learn to trust them once more. After training, the PAT dog will get to wear a special jacket on his visits and be part of a very rewarding organisation.

AGILITY

This is an exciting sport where a dog is trained to weave through poles and tunnels, jump over hurdles and many other obstacles, while the handler runs alongside. The times are recorded and prizes awarded. Agility teams from clubs compete against each other and, like dog showing, there are competitions on most weekends around the country. These remarkable dogs and owners can be seen at Crufts, entertaining the vast crowds in the main arenas. There are different-sized courses for all sizes of dogs. If you think this sport is for you and you can run and keep up with your dog, contact the Kennel Club for details of an agility club in your area.

FLYBALL

This is another exciting dog sport that you may well have seen at Crufts or Discover Dogs. Teams of dogs race the length of a course to retrieve a ball from a box that they trigger with their front feet before racing back to their handlers. Raced in relay teams it is fast, noisy and extremely exhilarating. Handlers do not have to be as fit as they would for agility competition but must have dogs willing to be trained to work the box and release the balls.

OBEDIENCE

This is one of the older canine hobbies and very impressive to watch. All dogs need some obedience training so why not go along to a basic class and see if you enjoy this sport? You can move up through the classes until you feel ready to join in with the competitions. Down stays, heelwork, retrieving items – it's amazing to watch and so satisfying when your own dog can follow commands and work with you.

HEELWORK TO MUSIC

Anyone who has seen heelwork to music demonstrations just before the Best in Show competition at Crufts will agree that the music and the extremely clever dogs can bring a tear to the most hardened viewers. This sport is now so popular that classes and demonstrations are springing up all over the country. Although it is akin to dancing, handlers just need to be able to control their dogs and be able to move around the show ring with their dog. Is it something you could do?

WORK IN THE DOG TRADE

A love of dogs and dog showing can take over one's life to the point that many people decide to change their occupation and work within the canine world. Those who have worked in sales and promotions move to work for dog food companies; some buy trade stands and follow the shows around the country selling their wares. Grooming parlours, pet shops, boarding kennels the list is endless. Scratch the surface of someone working in the pet market and underneath you will find an exhibitor. What could be better than your business and hobby working hand in hand?

JOIN THE KENNEL CLUB

Why not become part of the organisation behind your favourite sport? Although it takes time to become a full member of the Kennel Club, it is possible to be an affiliate member. A form can be downloaded from the Kennel Club website and for the cost of £20 per year you will have a subscription to the *Kennel Gazette*, which is the organisation's flagship publication, along with a loyalty card, access to discounted tickets to Discover Dogs and Crufts, invitations to Kennel Club open day tours, a pin badge, email newsletters and much more besides.

TAKE A CANINE COURSE

Why not try a distance-learning course? There are quite a few about our canine friends and as you can study at home and in your own time your obligations to your dogs can still be fulfilled. One educational establishment that is at the forefront of animal training courses is the Animal Care College overseen by principal

David Cavill, a well-known expert in the canine world. Why not start with a first aid course for pets or perhaps learn how to understand your family dog in more detail. With showing, judging and breeding courses as well as animal behaviour and alternative therapies, there is something for most canine enthusiasts to study. Visit their website for more information: www.animalcarecollege.co.uk

ENJOY YOUR HOBBY

Whatever you decide to do with your dog, it has to be enjoyed by both dog and owner. Perhaps for you and your dog a walk in the countryside is enough or a trip to the coast. As long as you and your dog have a great life together, it is time well spent. Add showing and it is a fantastic experience. Enjoy your dog and enjoy your showing!

Author's story

We chose to breed a few litters and enjoyed the experience very much. We have many friends connected through our love of our breed and our dogs are part of our everyday life. At present, many of our dogs are elderly and sadly will not be with us much longer. Yet we can look back on their lives and enjoy our time together and also remember those now at the rainbow bridge. Perhaps the worst part of owning a dog is having to say goodbye all too soon.

A good exhibitor...

Will enjoy a fulfilled life with their dog.

> ### A bad exhibitor...
>
> Will hopefully still love their dog regardless of their poor sportsmanship.

The Rainbow Bridge

For pet owners facing the loss of a pet the Rainbow Bridge has given much comfort. The author has never been known but to him or her we give our thanks. The Rainbow Bridge is where we all want to go to be reunited with our beloved pets when the time comes.

Just this side of heaven is a place called Rainbow Bridge. When an animal dies that has been especially close to someone here, that pet goes to the Rainbow Bridge. There are meadows and hills for all of our special friends so they can run and play together. There is plenty of food, water and sunshine, and our friends are warm and comfortable.

All the animals that had been ill and old are restored to health and vigour. Those who were hurt or maimed are made whole and strong again, just as we remember them in our dreams of days and times gone by. The animals are happy and content, except for one small thing; they each miss someone very special to them, who had to be left behind.

They all run and play together, but the day comes when one suddenly stops and looks into the distance. His bright eyes are intent. His eager body quivers. Suddenly he begins to run from the group, flying over the green grass, his legs carrying him faster and faster.

You have been spotted, and when you and your special friend finally meet, you cling together in joyous reunion, never to be parted again. The happy kisses rain upon your face, your hands again caress the beloved head, and you look once more into the trusting eyes of your pet, so long gone from your life but never absent from your heart.

Then you cross Rainbow Bridge together ...

(Author unknown)

Glossary

Agility: Action sport for dogs involving jumping, weaving and moving at speed.

Baiting: Rewarding a dog using pieces of food in the ring.

Benching: A wooden structure where a dog is kept safe at major dog shows when not in the ring.

Best of Breed: An unbeaten dog that is declared by the judge to be the best example of his breed on the day of the show.

Best Opposite Sex: A dog or bitch that is runner up to the Best in Show, or Best of Breed and is of the opposite sex to the winner.

Breed standard: A blueprint of each breed of dog held by the Kennel Club.

Catalogue: A book containing details of every entrant at a show including class entrants and ring numbers.

Challenge Certificate (CC): An award given to a dog at a championship show (where CCs are on offer) when it is the unbeaten dog or bitch in its breed. There are usually CCs for a dog and bitch in each breed, although it is now known for just one CC to be awarded in some breeds to the Best of Breed winner. Challenge Certificates are sometimes called tickets.

Champion: A dog or bitch that has won three Challenge Certificates from three different judges.

Championship show: A show where Challenge Certificates are on offer. This can be a general show, breed show or group show.

Class: Each breed has a number of classes allocated at a show. A class can be for a puppy through to an open class for champions and older dogs. When making an entry, state which class you wish to enter your dog into.

Companion show: A fun dog show, licensed by the Kennel Club where any breed or crossbreed may enter. There are classes for pedigree dogs and also fun classes for all dogs to enter on the day of the show.

Critique: This is a report written by a judge on all his or her winners. A judge is contracted to write a critique and send it to the canine press for publication.

Crufts: The biggest and best dog show in the world. The only UK dog show in which dogs have to qualify for entry. This show is organised by the Kennel Club.

Crufts qualifier: A class where certain places, if won, qualify a dog to enter Crufts the following year.

Dancing to music: An exciting sport where dogs accompany their owners making movements to music. This is one of the newer dog sports and is becoming very popular.

Exercise area: A ringed-off area at a dog show designated for dogs to 'do their business'. It is set away from the main area for cleanliness reasons.

Exhibitor: Someone who shows a dog at a dog show.

Exhibitor pass: A pass that is sent to an exhibitor so that they can gain entrance to a show with their dog.

Gait: The movement of a dog.

Going over: A term for when a judge assesses a dog in the show ring.

Group: Every one of the 209 breeds of dog recognised by the Kennel Club belongs to a 'group' depending on their traditional use. At a show organised on the group system, the Best of Breed winners will compete for Best of Group in their designated group.

Gundog group: One of the seven designated groups of dog. This is for dogs that traditionally worked to the gun.

Heelwork to music: See 'dance to music'.

Hound group: One of the seven designated groups of dog. This is for dogs that at one time hunted either by scent or sight.

Import register: Breeds of dog bred in another country and moved to the UK go onto a register if the breed is not yet recognised by the Kennel Club.

Judge: A person qualified to preside over an entry of dogs at a dog show. This person will have trained for this duty and have been passed to perform his or her duties by a breed club at open shows and by the Kennel Club at championship shows.

Junior warrant: An award won by dogs when they have won classes at open and championship shows and have the required number of points.

Kennel Club: The governing body for purebred dogs in the United Kingdom.

Limit show: A show limited to members of a club. This can be a breed club or a training club affiliated to the Kennel Club.

Line up: The row of dogs waiting to be assessed by a judge.

Match night: A competition night at a dog training club where an invited judge will preside over the members' dogs.

Not for competition: This is for dogs that are taken to a show but not entered in a class. Entries have to be made for these dogs on the entry form when the owner enters other dogs for competition.

Not separately classified: This is usually a class at general dog shows for dogs that do not have classes scheduled for their breed.

Novice: A dog that has not yet won three classes, puppy class not included.

Obedience: A sport for dogs where they have to perform movements or stay on command. This is an interesting sport to watch and join.

Open show: A show without Challenge Certificatess that is open to all dogs at general open shows or all levels of winning dogs at breed club events.

Order of judging: When showing you will always need to know the order of judging whether you are first or last in the ring. Larger shows will notify exhibitors ahead of the show. Open shows usually have the order of judging listed in the catalogue or on a poster at the show. Sometime the order of judging is published in the canine press.

Moving your dog: This when you walk or run your dog in the ring when told to by the judge. You will be informed where to run your dog and sometimes the required pace.

Name applied for (NAF): This has to be written next to the dog's registered name when completing an entry form if the Kennel Club has not yet approved the name of your dog.

Novelty class: A competition at a companion show entered for fun. This can be the prettiest bitch, dog with the waggiest tail or one of many other classes with funny names. These classes normally attract large entries and traditionally raise money for charity.

Pastoral group: One of the seven designated groups of dogs. Dogs in the pastoral group are traditionally herding dogs. This is the newest of the groups and was formed when the Kennel Club split the large working group in 1999.

Rare breed: A breed that has diminished in numbers or is fairly new to the UK and has not yet reached large numbers.

Reserve: In reference to awards, a reserve can either be the runner up to the Challenge Certificate winner or a fourth place in a class.

Results: This is a list of class and best of breed winners usually published in the canine press or online by show printers.

Ring: An area set out at a dog show where each breed competes. The ring is in fact square or rectangular.

Ring clip: A small pin with an attachment to which the ring number is clipped. It is worn by every exhibitor in the show ring.

Ring number: Each dog is given a unique ring number. This number is listed against the dog's name in the show catalogue and is worn by the handler. This is the only way that a judge recognises a dog. He or she cannot identify the dog's name until after the show when the numbers are compared to the catalogue. The steward marks the judge's catalogue in the ring so that judging is deemed fair.

Ring steward: A person who assists the judge in the show ring. A steward will call each class and check off the dogs as they enter the ring. He or she will also assist the judge by handing out awards and marking up the catalogue with the class placings.

Ringcraft: A training club where a dog and handler are taught dog-showing techniques. A ringcraft class can also be a social club for dogs and owners.

Rosette: A colourful ribbon award often handed to those people winning a place in each class. They are collected and admired by exhibitors.

Secretary: The secretary deals with all the paperwork for a breed club or show society, calls meetings and keeps minutes.

Seen dogs: These are dogs that have already been seen by the judge in a previous class and have entered another class at the show. They will be set to one side of the ring while the judge goes over new dogs. He or she will then assess all dogs before placing the winners.

Show lead: A special lighter weight lead used only in the show ring.

Show manager: A committee member who is in charge of the dog show.

Show schedule: A booklet that outlines details of a dog show from judges and breeds through to classes and prizes. An entry form is always enclosed with a schedule. It is now possible to download a show schedule from the websites of show printers and canine clubs.

Stacking a dog: This is the term for standing a dog in the show ring ready to be inspected by the judge.

Stakes class: An extra class at a show that can be sponsored by a business or person. Quite often the class attracts extra prize money and the winner can go on to further competitions and awards as winner of the year or show.

Stewarding: Stewarding is work within the show ring done by those other than the judge. Being a steward gives you an insight into how a judge picks the winners and has to be undertaken while people are training to be judges. There are normally one or two stewards in each ring so volunteers are often needed at shows.

Stud book: The Kennel Club stud book is produced yearly and lists all dogs that have won their stud book numbers, dogs who have won Challenge Certificates and other awards. These books are much prized as collectors' items.

Stud book number: A dog can be awarded a stud book number by winning a Challenge Certificate, a Reserve Challenge Certificate, a Junior Warrant or several other awards. A dog can only ever have one number although his name is entered into the stud book every time he wins another award. A stud book number is considered to be a sign of excellence in the world of show dogs and is much coveted.

Table dog: A table dog is any small dog that has to go onto a table to be assessed by a judge in the show ring. At table height the judge is able to see every point of the dog without bending low to the ground. Dogs are placed onto the ground when being moved around the ring.

Terrier group: One of the seven designated groups made up from hardy, smaller dogs that pursue animals such as foxes, badgers and rats over and underground.

Thrown out: This is a term for not being placed in your class. You are not physically removed from the ring by bouncers!

Tickets: Another name for Challenge Certificates (CCs).

Toy group: One of the seven designated groups that is made up mainly from small lapdogs.

Trade stand: Seen at most dog shows, these are businesses selling mainly canine equipment. These stands follow the shows around the country and are often owned by people who show dogs.

Transfer applied for (TAF): This is written after a dog's registered name on a show entry form if the new owner has not yet received his or her papers from the Kennel Club. Transfer of ownership must have been applied for before entering a show.

Utility group: This is one of the seven designated groups of dogs and is made up of all the breeds that do not fit into the other six groups.

Variety class: Variety classes are often extra shows listed at general open shows. Dogs can be entered even if they have breed classes listed in the schedule.

Wet weather tent: A wet weather tent is used at outside shows for judging in bad weather or if the sun is too hot. At the larger benched shows the wet weather ring is always situated as close to each breed's benching area as possible.

Working group: This is one of the seven designated groups and comprises dogs that traditionally worked for their owners either on farms or guarding and protecting stock or people.

Very highly commended (VHC): When classes are judged there are always winning places for five dogs. Very highly commended is the name for fifth place. On the rare occasions that classes have sixth and seventh places they are called 'highly commended' and 'commended'.

Veteran: A veteran dog is a dog that has reached its seventh birthday. Veteran classes at shows are for dogs over seven years of age and are always special classes to watch as we once again admire our favourite old show dogs.

Useful Information

The Kennel Club
1–5 Clarges Street
Piccadilly
London W1 8AB
Tel: 0870 606 6750
Fax: 0207 508 1058
Website: www.thekennelclub.org.uk

Our Dogs – weekly show publication and online dog forum
1 Lund Street
Trafford Park
Manchester M16 9EJ
Editor: Alison Smith
Email: alismith@ourdogs.co.uk
Tel: 0870 731 6500
Website: www.ourdogs.co.uk

Dog World – weekly show publication
Somerfield House
Wotton Road
Ashford
Kent TN23 6LW
Editor: Stuart Baillie
Email: editor@dogworld.co.uk
Tel: 01233 621877

Website: www.dogworld.co.uk

Dogs Monthly – monthly dog publication
61 Great Whyte
Ramsey
Huntingdon PE26 1HJ
Editor: Caroline Davis
Email: Caroline.d@dogsmonthly.co.uk
Tel: 08450 948958
Fax: 08707 662273

DEFRA Pet Travel Scheme
Website: www.defra.gov.uk

Higham Press Ltd – show printer that also publicises show results
New Street
Shirland
Alfreton
Derbyshire DE55 6BP
Tel: 01773 832390
Fax: 01773 520794
Website: www.highampress.co.uk

Canine Information Directory – show printer that also publicises
show results
Website: www.canineinfo.idps.co.uk

Fosse Data Systems Ltd – show printer that also publicises show
results
Tripontium Business Centre
Newton Lane
Newton
Rugby, Warks. CV23 0TB
Tel: 01788 860960

Fax: 01788 860969

Website: www.fossedata.com

Email: enquiries@fossedata.co.uk

Animal Care College – distance learning courses

Index House

Ascot SL5 7ET

Tel: 01344 636436

Website: www.animalcarecollege.co.uk

Index